How to Bury a King

with very ~~best~~ wishes,

Peter Hobson

HOW TO BURY A KING

Pete Hobson

Published by Zaccmedia
www.zaccmedia.com
info@zaccmedia.com

Published March 2016

ISBN: 978-1-911211-17-4

British Library Cataloguing-in-Publication Data
A catalogue record for this book is available from the British Library.

Back cover image: "Tomb of King Richard III (no 2)"; charcoal and chalk on
paper; 297 x 420 mm; Jane Lee / © Eleanor Jane Lee 2015.

Front cover:
Top front photo by Will Johnson
Lower front photo by Ian Davies

DEDICATION

This book is dedicated to Sue, who by not really believing it was all quite as important as many other people thought, kept me sane whilst it all happened, and then bore with my writing about it as well, as we travelled round the very beautiful and also very wet Highlands and Islands of Scotland.

CONTENTS

'RICHARD'

My bones, scripted in light, upon cold soil,
a human braille. My skull, scarred by a crown,
emptied of history. Describe my soul
as incense, votive, vanishing; your own
the same. Grant me the carving of my name.

These relics, bless. Imagine you re-tie
a broken string and on it thread a cross,
the symbol severed from me when I died.
The end of time – an unknown, unfelt loss –
unless the Resurrection of the Dead...

or I once dreamed of this, your future breath
in prayer for me, lost long, forever found;
or sensed you from the backstage of my death,
as kings glimpse shadows on a battleground.

Carol Ann Duffy CBE FRSL (b.1955), Poet Laureate
commissioned by Leicester Cathedral for the reinterment
of King Richard III

PLAN OF LEICESTER'S CATHEDRAL QUARTER

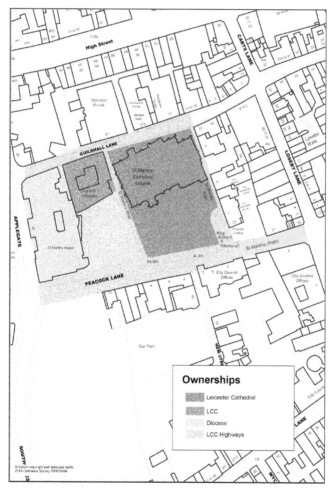

Plan shows land ownerships in greyscale. The car park
where Richard III was found in 2012 is behind
9 St Martins

ABOUT THE AUTHOR

Pete Hobson was born in 1953 in Macclesfield, and before being ordained worked variously as a demolition contractor, a postman and a hospital orderly. Since 1977 he has spent most of his life as a 'vicar', first in inner-city Manchester, then in Hackney and, since 2000, in Leicester. He is married to Sue: they have five children, and a goodly number of grandchildren too. Pete likes reading science and historical fiction, supporting Leicester Tigers, and a good walk, but not all at the same time.

FOREWORD

The remains of King Richard III now lie in the Cathedral of St Martin 100 metres away from where they have lain in Leicester since 1485. The site of the old Greyfriars Friary sits opposite the cathedral. This was to become probably the most famous car park in the world.

An army of people made the discovery and identification of King Richard possible. The media then portrayed a fight between Leicester and York as a Judicial Review ensued which was in fact a discourse in law about proper archaeological practice. When asked by Radio York whether I was up for the fight, I said it takes two to fight and we are not fighting! The judgment was one of the clearest I have ever read. We proceeded to plan for reinterment in March 2015 and to raise £2.5 million mostly from Leicestershire without help from the state.

Throughout the Project, Revd Peter Hobson was our lead cathedral staff member. We seconded him to help given his experience of major projects but also because we knew he would wish the core purpose of the cathedral to be embedded. Somehow, in the good purposes of God, this was to become part of our Christian mission.

Very often as the Dean I found myself at the eye of the storm, required to hold the process together so that everything would genuinely be marked by 'dignity and honour'. On many occasions Pete had to help us negotiate these tricky questions and convey difficult but clear decisions.

This book is a memoir. It is a recollection of two years of life and ministry. Others have already highlighted different aspects of the story with a definitive stance that doesn't always bear scrutiny. This is a very personal account with some new information which has not been shared previously. It will take many contributions to create an agreed history but if it is to be consistent with other aspects of Richard III's story, there is likely to be further debate.

King Richard III's motto carved on his tomb is Loyaulte me lie, which means 'loyalty binds me'. Alas for Richard, he suffered defeat due to the disloyalty of his friends. I can testify that Pete has been utterly loyal to this Project. Tens of thousands of people have already visited us. People will continue to be drawn into this history both ancient and modern. This memoir testifies to the fact that Leicester has done this well, with Pete as a vital player in our team.

Richard III, the defeated earthly king, now lies in peace. He faces east towards divine kingship and the Chapel of Christ the King in hope of the resurrection of the dead. This memoir records the practical journey we have undertaken but it also testifies to this eternal hope.

The Very Reverend David Monteith, Dean of Leicester
January 2016

PREFACE

There are many ways the remarkable story of the discovery and subsequent reinterment of King Richard III can be viewed, and many of them have already been told. This is mine. Others involved may well have different views on almost everything I talk about. My own view comes from the heart of Leicester Cathedral – the institution that was most intimately involved in the way the person at the centre of this utterly unique and unparalleled story was finally laid to rest.

Along the way I want to think about what it all means, as the dust settles. To me, who found myself at the heart of delivering it, to those who long dreamed of this day, and to those five million or more worldwide who looked in on it with amazement over a week in March 2015.

I will be taking as read the basic stories behind the story – that is, the genesis of the Looking for Richard Project led by Philippa Langley; the Greyfriars dig led by Dr Richard Buckley; and the amazing work done by scientists, mainly from the University of Leicester but also elsewhere, to establish beyond all reasonable doubt that the remains first uncovered on 25 August 2012 are indeed the mortal remains of Richard III, the last Plantagenet King of England, who was defeated and killed by Henry Tudor at the Battle of Bosworth on 22 August 1485, and buried in the monastic church of the Greyfriars a few short days after – a church destined to be demolished on the orders of Henry's son, Henry VIII, less than 50 years later, yet in whose ground those remains were to lie for 527 years until they were rediscovered in a million-to-one chance in the summer of 2012. All of this has been well covered in many other books and writings – but this is the story, as yet untold, of what happened next, as Leicester Cathedral was charged with the unique task of the reinterment of those royal remains.

Pete Hobson

CHAPTER ONE

A MOMENT IN TIME

It was 5.35 pm on a Sunday afternoon in late March 2015 and I was standing alone in the middle of Cathedral Gardens waiting for the arrival of a king. Not just any old king, but King Richard III, the last of the Plantagenet dynasty, and also the last English king to die in battle, surrendering his throne to Henry VII, the first of the Tudors, at Bosworth Field on 22 August 1485. His skeletal remains, recovered from beneath a car park against all expectation and odds over two and a half years earlier, had been placed into a coffin of English oak, and that morning had begun a journey from the University of Leicester via the location of his death, half a millennium earlier, and then back into the city, to the accompaniment of thousands of excited yet respectful onlookers, gathered from all four corners of the globe.

My job over the past two years had been to make sure, on behalf of the cathedral, that all the arrangements for this moment were right. I'd spent that day overseeing the final rehearsals and preparations and now I was standing in the space cleared between the cathedral, packed with its patiently waiting congregation, and serried ranks of spectators on the pavement opposite, who had been gathering since early morning. To my left was a plethora of journalists, corralled on their specially constructed viewing platform. To my right a small party of peers waited, led by the Queen's cousin, Richard, Duke of Gloucester (also King Richard's title before he had ascended to the throne). The arrival of the royal remains, covered live by TV around the globe, involved a complex pattern of handover activity and it was my job to make sure every part of that went just as planned and practised. The Bishop was ready. The Dean was ready. The royal party was ready. The voice in my earpiece was telling me the coffin was on time, as it traversed the streets of what had been medieval Leicester, on its way to Cathedral Gardens, where I was standing largely invisible in my clerical gear. And in those few short moments, I thought back to how it had all begun for me, two and a half years earlier, and marvelled at what I'd got myself into.

CHAPTER TWO

IT BEGINS ...

"They've found Richard," said the Dean. And at first all I could think was, "I don't know anyone called 'Richard' who's gone missing." Then I realised. It was Richard III. The last Plantagenet King of England. The archaeologists had found his remains. And – not that I then knew it – my life was about to change in a very big way.

It was 7 September 2012 and Viv Faull, Dean of Leicester, had called me into her office from my day job as Director of St Martins House, the former grammar school building which we'd opened as a Cathedral and Diocesan Centre. I'd been responsible to the Bishop and Dean since 2009 for the initial project of the purchase and conversion of the place and then, since it opened in January 2011, for running it – a fascinating mixture of community outreach base, conference centre, diocesan and cathedral administration, and offices for commercial let. I did recall a phone call some weeks earlier from a woman called Philippa Langley, who had clearly assumed I knew who she was (though I didn't – not then), asking if there was any chance of up to a dozen car parking spaces in St Martins House grounds during a forthcoming archaeological dig. Sadly there wasn't, nor did l realise at the time the significance another car park was to assume in the whole story.

Of course at the time the formal identification of the remains as those of Richard III was still months away, but already what was known – the battle wounds, the location of the burial and the scoliosis of the spine – made most people involved in the story pretty confident. And Viv explained to me that she had been in conversation with Philippa for some time, and had provisionally agreed that should the bones of Richard indeed be uncovered, they could receive due reburial in the cathedral – only 100 metres away, over the road from the location of the dig. Within a few days, using the medieval Guildhall next door, the university proudly announced their find to the world – in suitably cautious language, which was from the outset widely ignored.

So began a most extraordinary two and a half years for Leicester and its cathedral, culminating, on 26 March 2015, in the reinterment of those remains, in a manner calculated both to provide a permanent resting place, and reflecting the appropriate ceremonial due an English monarch, so conspicuously denied him first time around. And an extraordinary time for me personally, as before long I was charged with taking overall responsibility for overseeing all cathedral events and processes connected with that reinterment. This is the story of how that panned out.

CHAPTER THREE

CHANGES AT
THE CATHEDRAL

SEPTEMBER 2012 TO MAY 2013

Of course it didn't all fall into place immediately. From the dig's ending in mid-September to the following 4 February when the identification of the remains as truly those of Richard III could formally be announced, at a press conference at the university, a lot was going on with those who were to become our new colleagues and friends at the university. But back at the cathedral our own changes were afoot.

Unknown to most of us, by the time of the discovery Viv Faull had already accepted the nomination to become Dean of York Minster – second only in ecclesiastical prestige to Canterbury Cathedral. By November she had left Leicester for her new post, and the cathedral was plunged into vacancy at the very top. The way English cathedrals work is not widely understood, but broadly speaking the dean is in charge, in church terms ranking second only to the bishop of the diocese, whose seat of teaching (or *cathedra* in Latin) is the cathedral. A dean is appointed formally by the Crown, but in practice, after much consultation and due process, by the bishop. They then enjoy considerable independence of action: certainly no bishop is able to 'line-manage' his or her dean, a situation that has at times given rise to considerable creative tensions and not a little satirical and comedic writing down the years!

So the cathedral was left in the hands of the next tier of clergy, the 'residentiary canons'. One of them was the Sub-dean, and so it was that the Urban Canon, Barry Naylor, stepped up to hold the fort at this crucial time. Working with him was Johannes Arens, the Canon Precentor, responsible for cathedral music and worship, and David Monteith, the Canon Chancellor, alongside a team of lay cathedral staff. Leicester is one of the newest and smallest English cathedrals, only becoming one in 1928 as the new diocese was brought into being, and has no financial reserves of significance or historic endowments, and its overall staff team is correspondingly modest. But this team it was that had to initiate the planning that would take matters from archaeological discovery to national reburial. And all without an overall leader. So the appointment of a new dean, which can take many months, was hurried up. The consultations took place, the post was advertised and candidates shortlisted, and by mid-February it was announced that the internal candidate, David Monteith, had been appointed, and would take up his new post in May. That was good news to all who know David – a genial but shrewd Northern Irishman in his mid-40s, with already a good track record of church work in parishes such as St Martin-in-the-Fields, Trafalgar Square, and a large south London parish in South Wimbledon before coming to Leicester in 2009. He had already made his mark at the cathedral, and was well placed to take the lead in this most significant moment in its relatively short history as a cathedral, but much longer as the parish church of St Martin. Indeed at the time of Richard III's first burial over the road in the Greyfriars Priory in 1485, St Martins had already been a place of Christian worship for at least four centuries.

David's appointment was announced in early March 2013, and created an immediate further problem as a result. There was a major task before the cathedral – that of the reinterment of a king – but having filled the top job from within the team, a big gap opened up behind, and the clock was ticking! They needed someone to manage the reinterment project, answerable to Bishop and Dean. Someone who understood the strange world of the Church of England intimately, yet also someone who they could be confident could deliver on a project of the highest profile, within a defined time limit. And they needed them to start more or less at once. So it was that a few days later David, and Tim Stevens, Bishop of Leicester, approached me with a fascinating request. Rather than looking to immediately fill the Canon Chancellor vacancy created by David's promotion, would I consider joining the cathedral on a temporary basis, to lead the reinterment project?

I've often been asked since how I felt about taking on such a task. If ever there were a job in the church that you could say, "They didn't prepare me for this at college", that would be the one, and there are all sorts of ways to answer that, but oddly enough the first thing I felt was not excitement, nor even trepidation – but plain and simple annoyance. Because I was, to my mind, at a crucial stage in another project, and one which was far more obviously focussed on the Christian mission of the church than anything to do with medieval history, or modern primetime TV. St Martins House, completed on time and on budget, had only been up and running for a bare two years. The five-year Business Plan, put together with much scrutiny over the year prior to opening, had us moving from financial loss to surplus within three years, and we were on track to do that – but it had been a difficult and demanding task. We knew of no other diocese or cathedral that had attempted anything quite like it. I had appointed the team who worked under me, and they knew me and my ways of working. Could I just step away from all that, trusting that someone else, as yet unknown to any of us, could come in and keep things on track? So it took me a week or so, over the Easter period, to come to what felt like the very risky decision to accept the request. I did so, on the basis that this was one of those opportunities you could regret forever not taking, and it has been good to see that under its new leadership the work we did getting things under way at St Martins House has not only continued, but blossomed.

So it was that on 18 May 2013 David Monteith was commissioned as the new Dean of Leicester – and on 19 May I took on the title of Acting Canon Missioner, and the task of ensuring, on his and Bishop Tim's behalf, that Richard was safely reburied in our cathedral – on time, on budget and in a manner befitting the unique occasion it was to be. It was, in legal terms, a secondment from the body employing me to run St Martins House to work for the cathedral, and it was to be paid for by utilising the funds saved by not filling the vacant Canon Chancellor post for 12 months. It was to turn out that we were over-optimistic about the time needed.

In the meantime, the university had formally confirmed the identity of the remains as those of Richard III, and following on that Barry Naylor, as Acting Dean, had received a letter jointly signed by the Vice Chancellor of the University of Leicester, Sir Bob Burgess, and Leicester's City Mayor, Sir Peter Soulsby, formally requesting that the cathedral prepare to receive the remains for reinterment.[1] At about the same time, up in York a small group calling themselves the Plantagenet Alliance had been formed and were indicating their intention to challenge the plans for reinterment in Leicester, on the basis that, as Richard's collateral descendants, they should have been consulted and had

---

1   A copy of this letter is shown in Appendix 1. (p109)

they been they would have stated that his own wish was for burial in York. To be honest, a lot of people were saying a lot of things at the time, and I don't think we took it all that seriously. But in the event their protests crystallised in the form of a legal challenge, a request for Judicial Review of the exhumation licence and the manner of its implementation. And although it never seemed they had anything approaching a case, whether in law, in fact or in history – a judgment eventually upheld by senior law lords in the Court of Appeal – that challenge was to hold up the entire process for at least a year – and in the process extend my secondment from 12 months to two years.

CHAPTER FOUR

GATHERING THE TEAM

MAY TO JULY 2013

I've said this is the cathedral's story, but so far it may have sounded quite a bit like just mine. Of course nothing really gets done without a whole team of people being behind it, and I've already mentioned some of the key leaders: Bishop Tim, as overall diocesan leader, David, the Dean, Barry, the Sub-dean, and Johannes, the Precentor. During the early summer of 2013, the Richard III Project Core Team was assembled. This group met regularly every Monday morning until the reinterment was complete, and whilst many other people were involved in many other matters, from the cathedral's perspective this was the place where plans were both hatched and put into effect.

Recruited to the project along with me was clergy colleague Alison Adams. Alison had recently taken retirement from prison chaplaincy at nearby Glen Parva Young Offenders' Institute, and was looking to continue in ministry, but not needing a stipend. She'd been recruited mainly to help both the diocese and the cathedral in the area of social responsibility, which was where her chief work lay. Indeed, over the next two years she was to be the main mover in enabling the Bishop's Poverty Commission, which took evidence and produced findings on poverty in the area covered by the diocese, in a time when government policies of austerity were making a major impact on communities up and down the country. But Alison has a background in education, and so led for the Project on all the work we did in that area – not least enabling local schools and others to learn about Richard's story in the light of his reinterment.

Early on I had concluded we also would need a project admin assistant of some sort, and had persuaded Chapter[2] to allocate funds for such a post. We were very fortunate to be able to recruit Emma Wigley, who had just graduated from the University of Leicester in medieval history and music – and was already an ardent Richard III fan. Emma became a sort of alter ego for the two years we worked together, helping us deliver far more than we might have imagined possible: she is also very sharp on social media, and her astute prompting helped us negotiate a safe course as we managed to maintain both our presence and our cool amidst the minefields of Facebook, Twitter and the like.

The cathedral had an existing part-time fundraiser and marketing officer, Claire Recordon, who also became a key member of the Team working closely with our external consultant as it became clear we would need to raise and spend up to £2.5m to do all we needed to – more of that later.

The final key members of the Team came from the Communications sphere of our life. Liz Hudson, Diocesan Director of Communications, was already a good friend and colleague, and she, together with her colleague Keith Cousins, completed the heart of the group that met week by week for those two years.

---

2   A cathedral is run by a combination of bodies but the 'Chapter', presided over by the dean, is the main operational one. It consists of the senior clergy and a larger number of lay members, and meets approximately monthly to oversee both policy and practice.

Left to right: Alison Adams, Liz Hudson, Pete Hobson, Claire Recordon, Emma Wigley, Keith Cousins, David Monteith.

Others joined us for varying periods of time: initially Nick Carter, a former editor of the *Leicester Mercury*, advised on publicity and communications strategy, until that became a separate strand of work in its own right; Claire gained a colleague for her work for the final nine months, in Georgia May (also a University of Leicester graduate[3]); and also in the final months Johannes would often join us to update on the work of the separate Liturgical Group, and Rosy Fairhurst, recruited to the cathedral as Canon Chancellor in the autumn of 2014, also sat in as she assumed responsibility for the necessarily greatly increased number of volunteer welcomers and guides in the cathedral. It was a special joy to be able to work with Rosy again, as she had begun her clergy career as curate to the team I had led in Hackney Marsh, East London, back in the 1990s.

So that was the Team – but what was the work we needed to do in those early months? It was clear two things badly needed getting a grip on. The first was essentially practical

---

3 Georgia's application for the post stood out by her inclusion of a photo of herself dressed up as Richard III from a student event she'd attended.

and financial: what was the budget for this project, and where would it come from? The second was more philosophical, and in the end far more important: what exactly was it we were trying to do in this reinterment? And how would we know we had done it? Both of these needed answering at the highest level – but then delivering in very practical ways. And alongside this, it became increasingly clear the Judicial Review would demand significant attention, if not directly from the cathedral then most definitely from our partners in the university and city council. But before exploring how our answers to all of these developed, it would be helpful to explain how the Project was structured in this first year of its life.

From the very beginning the nature of the Project involved partnership. In the early days this was a matter of liaison between the different bodies that Philippa Langley had approached with her initial requests – mainly the city council and the University of Leicester. But once it had become clear that something uniquely significant had been achieved in the discovery of the remains, the whole exercise had necessarily moved up several degrees. By the beginning of 2013 an informal but strong partnership had been established between the university, the city and county councils, and the Bishop, the diocese and the cathedral (not the same thing, contrary to what most outsiders imagine). Another key member of this grouping was the Lord Lieutenant of Leicestershire, Lady Jennifer Gretton – the Queen's representative in the area. The principals of these bodies started meeting regularly, under the leadership of Bishop Tim and Sir Peter Soulsby, and once he was Dean, David Monteith joined them. But, crucially, they created what at that stage was called the Executive Group, chaired by David, which was charged with developing and then putting into play the necessary plans. This was composed of representatives from the partner bodies, with authority to deliver on planning and execution, and was chaired by David Monteith. It was this body I joined in May 2013 on behalf of the cathedral – and for the next 12 months it was this body which carried the main weight for joining up and overseeing the developing work. This was in practice carried out in various Working Groups, namely Events, Finance, Fabric, Liturgy, Communications, and Legacy.[4] The first two of these I chaired myself, and the next two were also cathedral-led, but all the groups were constructed so as to contain membership from each of the partner bodies – plus participation from members of the local branch of the Richard III Society. The Executive Group was meeting monthly, to receive reports from and steer the work of the Working Groups, which met more frequently as necessary.

This was the decision-making framework within which we could aim to address those key initial issues – of budget and purpose – and respond to the challenge of Judicial Review. And alongside all of that, how was the practical work to be done, of preparing the fabric of the cathedral itself and constructing a programme to mark the unique event of the reinterment of a medieval king in a 21st-century city? That's the stuff of the next chapter.

---

4   A chart detailing the structure at this stage can be found at Appendix 2. (p110)

CHAPTER FIVE

HOW DO WE DO THIS?

SUMMER 2013 TO SPRING 2014

I've said the Executive Group started meeting monthly. It was in this Group, reported to by the Task Groups, that we hammered out the details of how to do this thing. It was a privilege to be able to sit through many a meeting, as we fielded concerns and acknowledged pressures from all sides, yet determined to set and steer our own course to get the thing done – and done right.

What's it all about?

It was clear from the beginning both that this was a unique event and also that different people saw its uniqueness in their own, often quite different, ways. For the Looking for Richard Project, led by Philippa, it was mainly about properly laying back to rest the king they had devoted years of their lives to studying, and had at last found. But they now had to come to terms with the undoubted fact that a project that had begun as their baby, entirely under their control and with little outside interest, had grown into something of immense interest, but over which they had little or no direct control – although I would say that their voice and views were never less than very significant, and we would regularly remind people that without their persistence and dedication none of this would be happening.

For the university, the discovery and then positive identification of these royal remains was an amazing tribute to the skills and abilities of many of their staff – first on the initial dig, and then on the science that verified the identity of the remains. People such as Richard Buckley, Matthew Morris, Turi King, Jo Appleby and Kevin Schurer were to become household names in many places – along with many colleagues. By mid-2013 most of their work had been done, though the fuller DNA analysis continued for many months to come, and it was more a matter of following the usual university processes of publishing and peer-review – though in a very unusual set of circumstances!

For the city and county authorities, a story that had always been a part of the collective history of the place had suddenly forced itself centre-stage in a big way. The eyes of the world were indeed on Leicester and Leicestershire, and of course it was a very proper part of the roles of those with responsibility for the place to make the most of it – commercially and economically, as well as historically and in terms of image and place.

But for the cathedral, and the wider church, it presented a different set of questions: What is the role of the English established church in relation to the monarchy – and not just to the current holder of that place, but for one from half a millennium earlier? Having initially given a moral commitment, and subsequently accepting the provision of the exhumation licence for reinterment in the cathedral, how should that be carried out? This included very practical questions such as:

Where should the tomb go? What should it look like? And who is going to pay for it? But also the equally important but less tangible matters such as: What should the service(s) look like? Who will be invited? And how do we keep all the key stakeholders and interested parties engaged and happy? And behind all of that the inevitable question: How do we best handle the anticipated intense publicity and media coverage? Because a story which had started in the imagination of a few driven individuals had landed in the lap of a relatively small cathedral, but was now set to be acted out before the eyes of a watching world. And although it was indeed a partnership project, with input and decision-making from a number of significant bodies and powerful individuals, when it came down to it, the actual events the world would be watching would be focussed almost entirely on our cathedral. And that was my job to arrange.

We talked to and fro about all of this in the Exec, reporting back to the Principals' meeting. What was the story we wanted to tell, and how would we tell it? It was agreed we needed to construct a Key Messages document, incorporating all of the main partners' concerns and interests that could provide a firm foundation for all that would be said and done as the Project moved forward. Liz and I worked on the first drafts of that. At the same time the Events Group that I chaired was asked to come up with a Timeline of possible events – and in doing that it seemed only right to construct it around a narrative structure. A first version of that Timelines document was written that was to go through innumerable versions, but at the end was recognisably the same as the one we started off with in that early summer.

It was out of these processes, running side by side, that the strapline emerged that would take us through to the successful completion: "With dignity and honour". Like all such phrases, it makes no great claims to originality – but it did encapsulate,

*The version of the whole project logo
approved for use by the cathedral.*

in four short words, the touchstone of all else that was to be
planned and executed – and on the way helped us reject several
bright ideas that just didn't measure up to the tone we wanted
to convey!

'Dignity' speaks of what every human being should be
entitled to expect, in death as in life; and 'honour' recognises
that here we were dealing with the actual mortal remains of
one who in his person and day had signified the nation as a
whole, and even now had the capacity to stir the deepest of
feelings in the hearts of many who would be attending to all
we did and said. We did at a slightly later stage consider adding
a further key word to that pairing: 'and in *peace*'. This would
have responded both to the concerns expressed by many about
the fate of Richard's own eternal soul, but also recognised that
the Battle of Bosworth was not the last battle that was to be
fought along the way to achieving a final resting place for this
equally much-maligned and much-admired monarch. In the
end we settled for the two words and the virtues of brevity –
but whenever I have been asked to talk on the events, I have
naturally found myself speaking to all three.

How much should we spend?

Whilst the Project was clearly one with several key institutional partners, each of whom had their own internal financial processes and procedures, the heart of it was to be borne by the cathedral – which included the heart of the costs. And how on earth do you calculate those? A key part of the back-story of Leicester Cathedral is that it had been raised to that state in 1927 from that of a long-standing city parish church, with no endowments or reserves. As such, compared with the more historic and larger cathedrals, it had always struggled to meet its modest commitments just to keep going day by day and year by year. In May 2013, there existed only an initial draft budget – drawn up on the basis of what we were able to anticipate at the time. And even this was in any case money the cathedral simply did not have, so it was obviously going to be necessary to go out and find it. It was on that basis that the Diocesan Synod,[5] meeting in March 2013, had generously committed up to £500,000 from the rather more substantial diocesan reserves to the cathedral's use – but on the understanding that this was the absolute limit of what could be delivered from that source, and anything further would have to be raised from elsewhere. Moreover, this was not simply a 'blank cheque' grant, but had to be applied for with due reasoning as the process developed. So in May one of my very first tasks was to construct a basic set of anticipated costs, and a set of financial procedures to control expenditure, so that we could both make proper use of that £500,000 and see our way to understanding what more would be needed. This was put to Cathedral Chapter later that month, and approved – and so it was that I became budget manager for

---

5 The Synod is the governing body of the Diocese of Leicester as a whole, with control of all its central finances and budgets. It is separate from the cathedral, and has no direct control over it.

half a million pounds, a sum which was to rise in due course to two and a half million, as the full extent and scope of what was necessary became apparent.

Fabric

Behind this deceptively simple word lay a vast amount of work we were called upon to do, and in a time frame far shorter than cathedrals are used to operating within. The 'fabric' of a cathedral is a technical term, and alterations of any significance not only have to be approved by the Chapter, but also by a national body known as the Cathedrals Fabric Commission for England – or CFCE.[6] They will also seek the views of the local Fabric Advisory Committee, or FAC, which is independent of the Chapter.[7] Clearly, to insert the tomb of a medieval monarch into a cathedral was something that fell well within the province of CFCE to have to agree to – or not.

Fortunately, Leicester was already well down the road of conversations with CFCE about the cathedral and its surroundings before ever Richard III's remains were uncovered. Indeed, by September 2012 we were already well on the way to gaining their approval for the remodelling of the somewhat dingy and unprepossessing churchyard into the new, welcoming and more extensive Cathedral Gardens – work on which began in November 2013 and was marked with an opening ceremony on 6 July 2014. As part of those conversations we had also made it clear – to a broadly sympathetic reception – that successive deans and Chapters had expressed the view that the inside of

6   This is a government-appointed Commission, with a five-year life span, chaired during this period by Frank Field MP. It meets monthly to consider all sorts of requests for advice from Cathedral Chapters up and down the land and in the end issue decisions on them.

7   Certain lesser matters can be approved simply on the advice of the FAC. Broadly this depends on whether or not it makes a permanent alteration to the structure of the building.

the cathedral was badly in need of alteration as well. So when the additional idea of making space for a medieval monarch's tomb emerged, there was already a wider context of discussion involved, and initial architect's plans and drawings had been on the table for some time.

It's time to introduce to this story two more of the key people whose input was crucial to bring it to completion. The first of those is Mandy Ford, at the time vicar of two churches in a couple of Leicester's more deprived inner-city parishes of Beaumont Leys and Stocking Farm. Mandy was also chair of the FAC, mentioned above, and as such was also charged with chairing the Fabric Task Group set up in the spring of 2013. Mandy has a background in teaching, a degree in fine arts, and exceptional people skills. It helped that she and David had already worked very well together with me on the creation of St Martins House in 2009 to 2010 and the work towards creating the new Cathedral Gardens. Shortly before the actual reinterment in March 2015, Mandy took up a new post as a Cathedral Canon herself, south of the Thames in Southwark Diocese, but her influence and input to the Leicester project was incalculable, steering the designs and ideas through a whole host of processes and personalities.

The other key person was our lead architect, James ("Everyone calls me Josh") McCosh, from the London firm of van Heyningen and Haward. They, and he, had been appointed as advisors back in the early days of the Cathedral Square Project in 2008, and had worked on and off on reordering ideas since then. Josh is also a remarkable man – tall, laconic and immensely creative, with incredible attention to detail, all of which was crucial to our progress. In addition he had the ability to play around with concepts in his sketchbook, so that we could discuss an idea at a meeting in Leicester, and on the train back to the office he would have pulled together half a dozen versions of it, and a recommendation on what was the best one to achieve what we had all said we wanted – but weren't quite sure how to do. He also, of course, had a great team behind him at the office, many of whom we got to know well, not least Yuli Lee who managed the entire construction contract, before giving birth days after the reinterment service. Josh had good contacts when it came to engaging the other professionals needed to transform a cathedral in quick order – quantity surveyors, structural engineers, mechanical and electrical consultants, and so on and so forth. Later on, he found us our stonemason James Elliott, who at the right time delivered a tomb and an altar against intricate design and impossible time constraints. But again that's a later part of the story.

There was considerable controversy over the design of the tomb, not least because, in this as in other areas, the ideas of the Looking for Richard team clashed with the processes and thinking of the cathedral. Here, as elsewhere, the considerable media-pulling-power of Philippa Langley, as principal originator of the whole process, meant that any ideas she opposed were certain to gather large headlines, and any pronouncements she made were sure to stoke strong emotions in the minds of the many who saw the entire project through the lens of her thinking. Long before any digging had begun, Philippa and her colleagues had prepared a comprehensive paper outlining their thinking, including a design for what they thought the tomb should look like – perhaps in the mistaken impression that the cathedral could simply accept it 'off the shelf'. But even had we wanted to, the complex processes of CFCE would have to have been followed, and in the event their faux-medieval design was not at all the sort of thing we felt was right for our cathedral. Given the anticipated numbers of visitors to this tomb for perhaps centuries to come, we were clear the principal imagery needed to speak of core Christian beliefs of hope in the face of death – which would of course have been central to Richard's own thinking in his day. So whilst images and words associated with the man himself should have a place in any tomb, it would clearly be secondary to the central Christian message.

So, guided by CFCE advice, Chapter approved its own Tomb Brief on 13 March 2013, suggesting what was needed was a below-ground interment, marked by a simple design for a 21st-century monument to a 15th-century monarch, and that all options should be considered 'for a gravestone, tomb or marker, including commissioning a new ledger stone or other appropriate memorial'. This took account of the existing ledger stone, which had lain flat in the floor of the chancel since 1982.[8] Our proposal was met with a public outcry, not all of it reasonably expressed. True to its brief of being flexible, listening and responsive, the Fabric Group allowed its thinking to develop and asked Josh and his team to produce some ideas responding to the brief but allowing for the monument to be raised above floor level. Josh came back with a design for a large block of stone placed above a brick-lined vault, the stone itself to be deeply incised with the primary Christian symbol of the cross – and with the secondary imagery relating to Richard himself placed on the surrounding floor.

Along with the tomb design came the question, arguably of much larger importance, as to where in the cathedral it was to go, and how would this fit into the wider reordering

---

8   The ledger stone had been donated to the cathedral by the Richard III Society at a time when no one was clear what had ultimately happened to Richard's remains, so it referred to him as simply having been "buried in the Church of the Grey Friars in this parish".

that now became not only desirable but essential. This was the
scheme which Josh had been working on already for a couple
of years, and which involved largely unpicking a scheme put
in during the 1920s as St Martins gained its cathedral status,
and generally named after the architect of the day, Sir Charles
Nicholson. The centrepiece of his scheme had been the creation
of a Chapter House[9] *inside* the new cathedral, composed of a
series of ornate wooden screens, which effectively sealed off the
central part of the building from ordinary worshippers. In the
process of digging into the thinking of the time we discovered
that Charles Nicholson and the then Provost, Frederick
MacNutt, had only expected his scheme to have a maximum
life of 60 years, before a new cathedral would have been built
– a project finally abandoned after the Second World War. So
the Nicholson screens had already outlived their expected life
span by some three decades! In 1982 the ledger stone had been
put towards the eastern end of that Chapter House area. We
wanted to locate the tomb of Richard III in roughly the same
place, and to do so by moving the large front wooden screen
back one bay, so also opening up the centre of the cathedral
under the tower to the congregation. To make such significant
changes to a cathedral involves all sorts of consultation with
official bodies such as English Heritage, the Twentieth Century
Society, the Victorian Society, and others. This can't be short-
circuited, and as you may imagine their views tend to be
weighed towards preservation of what is, and against change
to what might be. And, like us, none of them had previous
experience of what difference the presence of a medieval king's
tomb ought to make.

---

9   The Chapter House is, historically, where the Cathedral Chapter would meet,
and in medieval times it was a place of great significance. In the 1920s it was clearly
still assumed this was one of the things that marked out a church as a cathedral –
and as there was no land outside on which to build it, it had to go right in the middle
of the place!

All of this was discussed by the Fabric Group and then presented on 17 July 2013 to a consultative meeting at which were invited members of both CFCE and FAC, representatives of the Richard III Society and the other key stakeholders, including Leicester's own Civic Society and all our local MPs, who were by then getting very excited about the possibilities. The outcome of that day was a further round of design development, leading to the actual proposals that needed to be submitted to CFCE by mid-September, if they were to be published for public comment and then considered at their November meeting.

It was very tight going, not least working alongside most people's own summer holiday plans, but we did it, and got together a paper drafted by Josh, read over and agreed by David, Mandy and myself, presented to Chapter for their approval on 10 September and submitted forthwith to CFCE to meet their deadline. It showed a tomb designed of lightly coloured Swaledale fossil stone, placed on a base made up of the white rose of the House of York, encircled in black by Richard's name, dates and personal motto, *Loyaulte me lie* ('loyalty binds me' in medieval French) and also including four figures of a boar, which was his personal insignia. We were proposing that the monument be located in the area where the ledger stone currently lay, but behind a screen, relocated to form a new area to be called the ambulatory. We also had to show how this related well to a much larger scheme for the full reordering not only of the cathedral's east end but of the building in its entirety. The last thing we wanted, or that CFCE would have allowed, was for us to come back a few years later and look to redo any part of what we had now put in place. But before we can go any further on the story of tomb design, it will be important to pick up on the vexed question of the Judicial Review.

Our first design for the tomb in its setting.

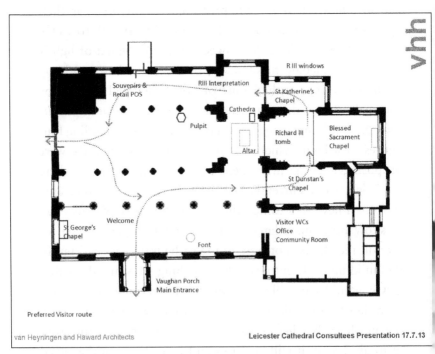

Plan showing how the proposed tomb location fits within the cathedral

Legal challenges

When the Plantagenet Alliance first lodged their protests none of us could believe it should be taken with too much seriousness. They were good at seeking publicity, it was true, and could count on the full support of at least two of the original Looking for Richard Project team – though not Philippa herself, who was more circumspect on her pronouncements on *where* he should be laid. But could they seriously think that up to 17 million collateral relatives of Richard, after five centuries had passed, deserved to be consulted over where he should be buried? And that such an immense undertaking and precedent should overturn all accepted procedures, and the legal licence for exhumation, which had explicitly specified Leicester Cathedral for reinterment, should the remains of Richard III be identified? But early in August, acting in the capacity of 'Duty Judge' during the long summer legal recess, Justice Haddon-Cave had ruled that the case at least deserved its day in court to be argued out – a day which was then set for 26 November 2013. That meant a lot of work for a few lawyers, but, more worryingly, a total hold on any of our public planning – because people could quite properly say that the whole matter was now thrown into legal doubt. We took the view that the fact there was to be a Review, whatever might be its outcome, could not overturn our present obligation to be ready to do what we had agreed to, and that it would be irresponsible of us not to continue to plan to carry out what we were legally obliged to do – and to do so by 31 August 2014, if the original terms of the licence were to be met. So we pressed on in our preparations.

I learned a lot about legal niceties in the course of the whole thing, including attending, on behalf of the cathedral, every minute of the three days of legal arguments presented in the

Royal Courts of Justice on the Strand before three High Court judges.[10] That was a strange experience. The outside view of the steps of the Courts are familiar from many a news item, and the insides to the viewers of TV legal dramas, but to find myself sitting in Court Room 5 awaiting the arrival of the legal team and the Bench of three was something else.

To try and put the matter as simply as possible: it is not possible for archaeologists to exhume bodies without a licence from the Ministry of Justice, and so such things are routinely issued all the time. The Alliance were arguing against the terms of this particular licence issued to the University of Leicester, which had allowed the exhumation of up to six bodies, and if one of them turned out to be Richard III, to reinter it in Leicester Cathedral. Other provisions were made for other exhumed remains. And it wasn't, of course, the exhumation itself they objected to, but the provision for reinterment in the cathedral. So the defendants in the case were the Ministry, who had issued the licence, and the university, who had applied for it. The cathedral was not a defendant but was named as an 'interested party' – which we most certainly were.[11] So although we decided against being legally represented, not least on the grounds of cost, we did submit Witness Statements, outlining the preparations we were making 'at risk' – statements which I drafted, although they were finalised by our lawyers and submitted by David Monteith as Dean.

10   The senior judge presiding was Lady Justice Hallett. She was assisted by Mr Justice Ouseley and Mr Justice Haddon-Cave – who had originally given the matter leave to proceed to a court hearing. Interestingly he was not initially named to take part in the hearing, but was then swiftly added to the first two. I speculate that having allowed the ball to be set rolling, he perhaps felt a special interest in seeing what the outcome might be, and asked to be allowed on to the team hearing the matter – but clearly as the most junior of the three.

11   As was York Minster, the burial place of choice of the Alliance. To their credit, the Minster took no formal interest in the proceedings, saying they were content to leave the matter to the Leicester authorities. Viv Faull, as Dean there, took a lot of personal abuse for this, from a few individuals, one of whom was subsequently convicted in court for some of his actions.

In that first hearing of November 2013 I attended on my own, and chose to sit just behind the Plantagenet Alliance's legal team, whilst the back rows were filled with their supporters, and also Philippa Langley and others of the Looking for Richard Project, and to my right were the representatives of the council and university. It was fascinating to see the boxes of papers being wheeled in and observe the interplay of solicitors and barristers. David was back in Leicester in a Bishop's Staff Meeting, and every so often I would text him updates on progress – and pretty soon a massive spanner was thrown into the works.

The city's legal team had submitted some last-minute papers, arguing that despite the clarity of the licence they should also be admitted as an Interested Party, on the grounds that they had a formal interest in the care and disposal of the remains. This was based on the fact they were found on land owned by the city council, and on an approach to the whole issue grounded in best practice for ancient human remains which are to be displayed in museums. Behind the scenes I'd been aware that this difference in approach between the city and university teams had been rumbling on – but no one had expected it to emerge like that. I'd seen a draft of this submission, a day or so before it was sent, and had instantly alerted David, and we'd tried to make more senior colleagues in City Hall aware of the problems it would produce, but by the time we had gained their attention we were too late to have any effect – the document had already been sent. So it was that in court Gerard Clarke, barrister for the Alliance, was able to argue that if the city was now claiming, at the last minute, some form of legal responsibility for how the remains should be disposed of, they surely ought not only to be an Interested Party, but an additional Defendant. It didn't take long for the Bench to agree! And the whole hearing was adjourned to a date to be determined to give all parties time to adapt to this new development – a date which ended up being four months later in March.

We'd been confidently expecting a rapid resolution of the whole matter, and this threw a real spanner in the works. As soon as the Bench retired, a flurry of conversations broke out both inside the courtroom and in the corridors outside, and phone calls were being made, as the news filtered out that far from getting the answer we needed, the whole matter had been kicked back into the long grass. In the next few days there was activity at the most senior levels of the Partnership, resulting in a dramatic change of tack from the council. A new legal team was appointed, and it was made crystal clear that the whole museums-based approach was fundamentally misplaced, when what was at stake was the responsible reinterment in consecrated ground of the remains of an identified individual.

When this did come back to court on 13 and 14 March, Liz Hudson and I both attended the re-run of the arguments on behalf of the cathedral. The city's new approach now mirrored the university's old one, which they had temporarily stepped away from, and was successfully argued by their new legal team and it was rapidly agreed the City of Leicester had never had any legal rights in the matter of a decision as to the place of reinterment.

Mr Gerard Clarke laid out the Alliance's case and it became increasingly clear from the questions from the Bench that he was not persuading the three judges at all. After that, Counsel for the Ministry of Justice (a senior QC) and for the university proceeded to rebut any and all arguments, and were clearly getting a much better hearing. This was real courtroom drama! And there was still time for one more twist. Just as Mr Clarke was getting into his stride an impassioned cry came from the public gallery at the back: "No! That's not right!" All eyes turned to the rear row of seats, where a tall, blonde woman was trying to make herself heard. Lady Justice Hallett clearly took a very dim view of this, and was about to order the offender removed, when it dawned on her who this woman might be. None other than Philippa Langley – who had taken exception to some things said by Mr Clarke and felt she needed to more fully inform the Court of the truth of the matter. After quick deliberation an exception to normal procedure was allowed, and Ms Langley was given the opportunity to write down the substance of her thoughts in a note, which was handed to the Bench. There then followed a five-minute recess, during which the note was shared with all leading Counsel, after which arguments were resumed. The rest of us in court never knew exactly what Philippa had written down, nor quite what it was she insisted the Court hear, but whatever it was, it never surfaced again in any of the arguments put forward. But it was a reminder, if one was needed, of the strength of feeling of those who had first gone looking for Richard – and how far we had travelled both in discovery and in process since their Project had been conceived.

In the event by mid-morning of 14 March all arguments had been exhausted and the hearing was ended. It seemed clear to all in court that there could only be one outcome.[12] But it still took a long, painfully agonising wait until on 23 May the formal judgment was handed down, confirming conclusively what we had reckoned all along – that there were no grounds for contesting the licence and its application, and that all the preparations we had been making in good faith, but at risk, could now proceed. It had all been one huge sideshow, fated never to succeed, which had no doubt greatly excited any

---

12 However, we had to appear neutral and respect the Court's processes. So outside I was pressed by a succession of TV reporters to express myself "very happy with the outcome" but took refuge in the time-honoured, "Quietly confident, but we'll have to wait and see."

number of casual onlookers, but from our point of view had simply added unnecessary delay – and so cost.

Tomb and cathedral designs – revisited

The date first set for the judicial hearing had been 26 November – less than a week after the date when CFCE were due to consider our plans at their monthly meeting on 21 November. What we were hoping for was approval in principle of our proposals by CFCE, followed by dismissal of the Judicial Review the following week. It didn't happen like that at all. I was on holiday for the week of the CFCE meeting, but David, Mandy and Josh all travelled to London for the day. We had discovered that although normally only paper submissions were considered, it was also possible to present your ideas in person. We had asked for and been granted that right. The proposals had been published in September and were open for public comment – and CFCE had found themselves on the end of an unprecedented lobbying campaign, receiving well over 500 submissions and emails on the matter, many repeating word for word a pro forma letter, published to her supporters by Philippa. These strongly objected to the design of the incised cross in the Swaledale tombstone, whilst broadly welcoming the other aspects of the design, including the Yorkist rose on the floor. David and the others felt they got a fair hearing before CFCE, but then had to retreat and await the outcome. In the meantime, the following week I had gone to London to be the face of the cathedral in the courtroom and witnessed the strange goings on outlined above, resulting in an open-ended adjournment of the hearing, until all the parties could get their respective ducks in a row. It was a week or so later that we received the formal letter from CFCE telling us that, far from what the objectors had argued, they welcomed the raised part of the tomb design, but that they were not at all convinced by the large white rose on the floor. Too fussy, they thought. Needed to be simpler. We should think again. They were also clearly anxious not to be seen to be presuming on the outcome of Judicial Review – so declined to issue any final verdict on the tomb as a whole until that had been resolved in our favour. The good news, however, was that they liked the overall reordering 'master scheme', and within it the proposals for creating the ambulatory. But even there they felt more could be done to allay the concerns of the heritage lobby about the impact of largely dismantling Sir Charles Nicholson's scheme. So back to the drawing board it was, irrespective of Judicial Review.

A further intensive period of thinking and consultation followed over Christmas and New Year, and a redesigned tomb emerged from Josh. This time the questionable floor design was removed, and the elements particular to Richard placed on a black plinth, on which the main tomb would sit. We consulted all parties again in February – and got a broadly positive response. We also made contact with the author of the acknowledged definitive study of the work of Sir Charles Nicholson, a clergyman working in the depths of East Anglia called Edward Bundock. He visited the cathedral at our invitation, and Josh and I spent a day showing him what we had in mind and asking his views. He then wrote a report which thankfully fully endorsed our proposals regarding moving the screens and losing the seating behind them.[13] This became a further appendix to our renewed submission to CFCE, which was on the agenda for their meeting on 20 March – just a week after the Judicial Review final hearings but before any ruling had been issued. We felt caught in an enormous game of chicken

---

13 Later, when the fixed canons' seating was removed as part of the works, we agreed that some of them could be reinstated in one of Edward's East Anglian churches.

The final tomb design, as eventually approved by CFCE.

and egg. Would CFCE give us permission to carry out the plans we had developed with them, or would they once again defer pending legal processes?

Once again David and Mandy travelled down to present the case. Once again they were well received. And then, only days later, I got the good news by phone call, followed by letter: CFCE had formally approved our revised plans. In fact they had been very impressed by our processes and ways of working. There were conditions, of course – there always are – but providing we got a legal green light, we were good to go.

Funding – the story develops

Meanwhile, the whole question of what this would all cost and how we paid for it continued to exercise our minds. All the delays had, of course, increased design and development costs. Architects and allied trades don't come cheap – and to get this right we had to not cut corners. Then there was the question of the ticking clock on my job. I had been seconded initially for 12 months due to end by 31 May 2014, by which time we had initially thought it would all be done and dusted. The cathedral had covered my salary costs for that one year from the funds attached to the job of Canon Chancellor, but now needed to press on and appoint someone to the substantive post. We would have to roll my salary costs after that point into the developing budget. Then, as well as the tomb and reordering, there were other things Chapter was anxious to do to make the whole look and work right, not just for Richard's tomb, but also for our on-going life as a cathedral. We needed a new altar-table, to sit in the new sanctuary under the tower. We could do with new sanctuary furniture to accompany that. The choir had previously sat in the Chapter seats, or on ordinary chairs in the nave, so new choir stalls were needed. We should have new canons' seats for when the Cathedral Greater Chapter needed to meet formally. And above all we needed a new cathedra. That's where the bishop traditionally sits,[14] and from which every cathedral gets its name. It's an actual seat – and the one Nicholson had given us back in 1927, a magnificent piece of joinery as it was, was now hopelessly out of place. It sat in the old sanctuary at the east end, putting the bishop far out of sight and mind for almost all practical purposes, and it reached grandly up to the skies, almost like a space rocket, with two sidecars, as no one then could conceive of a bishop without liturgical attendants. It said all the wrong things about bishops and people and God for a 21st-century cathedral. Bishop Tim had never liked it and hardly ever used it. Surely now was the time to get on and replace it with something more modern and fit for our purposes? But all of that would, of course, incur costs as well. So into the budget process it went.

The question of how to raise whatever sum we eventually decided upon was also pressing. The uncertainty caused by Judicial Review had meant that it was effectively impossible

---

14 Most especially when teaching the Christian faith – hence the saying of someone speaking 'ex cathedra' – literally 'from the chair' – meaning 'speaking with great authority'.

for us to mount any sort of public appeal until we could say, hand on heart, we knew we were going to do this thing. Our partners had all had their own costs, of course – not least the university with the dig itself, followed by all their scientific work on the remains – and in a time of austerity none of them were disposed to be giving public money to a cathedral for what was, when all was said and done, largely going to end up benefitting the fabric of the building itself. It was clear this was not a task we should attempt unaided and we decided to seek out a fundraising consultant to help us along the way. After sounding out in various directions we interviewed three, and appointed Christine Stokes, who hails from South Wales. Christine was genuinely excited about the Project in its own right, and had a good record of raising large sums of money for other projects – including the previous Rugby World Cup. I became her 'handler' for the cathedral and, working with David as Dean, Bishop Tim and others in our system, she helped us draw on existing contacts and goodwill, and find new ones that would be so captivated by the project for the reinterment of a medieval king that they would themselves be willing to help make it happen. Christine worked with us from autumn 2013 until the reinterment itself, on a paid basis, and her advice and experience were key in enabling us eventually to realise every penny we needed – and a bit more besides – and has become yet another person I'm so glad to have met and worked with.

So it was that by January 2014 our developing budget was approaching £2m, and still incomplete, and we were ready to launch our Appeal Website – 'kingrichardinleicester.com'.[15] It contained a letter from the Dean – of course – and one from the Patron of our Appeal. For that purpose we had been able

---

15 This site later developed into a place for the whole Project, working along with all our partners, and a new site was created specifically for the duration of the Cathedral Appeal.

to secure the support of the Queen's first cousin, Richard, Duke of Gloucester, who for many years had also been patron of the Richard III Society. Richard III was himself Richard, Duke of Gloucester from his teens until crowned king, and the present Duke has a lifelong interest in his namesake. This enabled us to develop one element of our 'controlling narrative' about the reinterment, that of reconciliation. The Wars of the Roses were effectively ended by Richard's defeat and death in 1485 at the hands of Henry Tudor, who went on, as Henry VII, to found the famous Tudor dynasty so beloved by fans of English history the world around! These vicious wars, also called the 'Cousins' Wars' because they so often pitted noble cousin against noble cousin in brutal battle and ruthless coup, were brought to an end at Bosworth Field. We wanted to offer some reconciling note to history, by bringing together in amity at the reinterment the current senior representatives of all those noble families who had fought that day, or in the wars of that time.[16] Christine helped us develop this idea, and to secure the support of the Duke of Gloucester to that end was of considerable value. And in the end we did it – at the service of reception of the remains, the Duke walked behind the coffin, followed by two representatives from the House of Lancaster and two from the House of York, who formally laid the pall onto the coffin as the service proceeded. And at the reinterment itself four days later seventeen representative 'Bosworth peers' were assembled, to bear witness to the laying to rest not only of Richard's remains, but of the enmity that had surrounded his death.

The final element of the website was the regularly updated 'inside story' of the campaign as it developed. So began 'Pete's

---

16 These were what we came to call our 'Bosworth Peers'. Most are current holders of noble titles, often but not always the exact title as in medieval times. They were carefully researched on our part, with the help of the College of Arms, itself founded by Richard in 1483.

Blog',[17] a regular sideways look (I aimed at weekly and didn't always manage it) at what was going on, and what I was thinking about it all. The first came out on 31 January 2014, and was centred on the talk the comedian and actor Sanjeev Bhaskar had given in his capacity as Chancellor of the University of Sussex at our daughter's graduation the previous week, and the final one, titled *#richard reburied – he is now,* was published on 28 March 2015. Taken together they give a particular insight into the final year or so of the Project, and I have to say they did lead me into a fair bit of correspondence over the year or so they ran, which further opened my eyes to the depth of feeling that this most extraordinary of monarchs still commands!

---

17   Later renamed 'Cathedral Blog' – but in the event almost all of them were written by me! There's a list in Appendix 3. (p111))

CHAPTER SIX

THE GREEN LIGHT

SUMMER 2014

Now we had the green light to proceed – and several things had to happen, and happen fast. And to do that we badly needed extra help. So it was that the whole project moved up a gear, two new people were added to the overall team, and a restructuring of the organisation took place. From the city council, Miranda Cannon was seconded for two days a week as overall Project Director. Miranda was a senior officer with a winning personality, tons of experience in running large projects, and a readiness to work with the wide range of partners already up and running. And Julian Haywood, seconded full-time from the county council,[18] became Project Manager, ably inserting himself into the middle of a project already well under way and enabling all of us to continue to deliver effectively and in good spirits. Julian was welcomed to occupy a desk in our cathedral office, in what had more or less become 'Project HQ', and for a year was a valued honorary member of the cathedral team!

The Project also reshaped itself, so the existing Exec committee became a Project Board and working to it, instead of

---

18   Where he had been heading up their Customer Service team. Useful preparation for what he found himself in the midst of, as he was heard to comment!

the former Task Groups, were six Workstreams. The Principals' group had the previous autumn turned itself from an informal consultation into a formally constituted body, the Cathedral Quarter Partnership, chaired jointly by Bishop Tim and Peter Soulsby, which retained overall control and strategic direction.[19]

I now found myself in charge of a Cathedral Workstream whose remit was expanding dramatically in all directions. Other Workstreams included Events, Communications, Civic and Ceremonial, and Legacy, and it was part of Julian's job to make sure they all worked together well. We were all interacting with each other, but my main focus had to be on getting the cathedral itself ready for the central part it was to be called upon to play, and it felt good to be able to concentrate my energies in one clear area. This included getting all the building alterations completed to time; making sure a tomb of the agreed design was in place; ordering and obtaining the agreed additional items – cathedra, altar-table, liturgical seating and choir stalls; helping the liturgical group plan and deliver a range of services for something no one had ever done before; and overseeing the raising and spending of £2.5m to do all of that. All the time also playing my part in fielding a steady stream of comments from all directions, most of which were aimed at persuading us we had got something – or everything – all wrong, and some of which were happy to do so in the most forthright of terms. This included some very delicate negotiating with the Richard III Society and the Looking for Richard Project team over a whole range of matters where still we had apparently not performed as expected.[20]

---

19   The revised Project Organisation Diagram can be found in Appendix 4. (p113)
20   It is worth noting that we developed a very good working relationship with Dr Phil Stone, the chair of the Society, and Wendy Moorhen, his deputy, who often found themselves caught between the widely varying expectations and hopes of their many members and the realities of what was possible. That we achieved everything in as positive a way as we did is as much a tribute to their leadership of the Society as it is to anything else.

Setting the date

The original licence had given what must have seemed like a reasonably generous two years to plan for that reinterment by 31 August 2014. But the delay caused by Judicial Review had clearly put paid to all of that. Whilst we would have been neglectful of our duty if we had made no plans, we also couldn't be seen to prejudge a judicial process, and in any case it wasn't possible for the cathedral to seriously carry out fundraising in that situation.

Richard Buckley applied to the Ministry of Justice for an extension to this timeline, which was granted with no fuss. In the process of that we discovered that we also needed legal permission to reinter remains within the cathedral – which had been closed to burials since the mid 19th century.[21] So I quietly drafted a letter to the Ministry asking for permission for just one more burial to be allowed within the cathedral itself – that of King Richard III. This had to be submitted to the Privy Council, and fortunately was also granted without fuss – and I have the paperwork to prove it!

So by the end of May 2014 we had a green light from all directions: we now simply needed to get on and do it. We had reckoned all along on needing some six months for building works, and I argued strongly that if we got a move on we had just time to complete the work, to prepare for the services and to carry out the reinterment the right side of Easter 2015. This was important because 6 May was set as the date not only for a General Election, but also, locally, for the next election to the post of City Mayor,[22] both of which were sure to present major distractions. Those most actively involved discussed the

---

21 Ironically whilst we had realised this was the case for York Minster, though not made anything of it, it was only confirmed it also applied to Leicester at this stage – as indeed it was true of other English cathedrals.

22 Leicester had become one of the first cities outside London to have an elected executive Mayor when Peter Soulsby was elected in 2011 for his first four-year term.

options, and a paper was submitted to the Partnership Board proposing a reinterment date some ten days before Easter – so allowing the cathedral to celebrate Holy Week and Easter, the heart of the Christian year. The dates were accepted, and we then knew what we had to do – get the cathedral ready for a reinterment with dignity and honour on 26 March 2015.

Preparing the cathedral

By the time the High Court decision was announced we had had our plans provisionally approved by CFCE for some two months, and Josh and his team were well advanced in turning those into a practical package to put out to tender. We drew up a shortlist of possible contractors, knowing that we had to strike a balance. We needed a firm skilled in conservation works – a specialist area in itself. They needed to be big enough to do the job reliably – and we knew they would have to work to a very tight deadline. Also ideally we wanted the firm to be as local as possible – a principle we'd tried to follow throughout the Project at all levels, though never at the cost of not going for the best quality work as well.

A matter of no little concern to Chapter was the fact that we had to place an order for a building contract worth in the region of £700,000 (inclusive of VAT), plus all related professional fees, which was due to be paid for by the outcome of an Appeal that we had only just been able to launch! This difficulty was resolved by the generous provision of an underwriting facility, provided jointly by the city and county councils, and the Samworth Family Foundation. They were able to promise us up to £1m between them to be drawn down as and when needed to cover in the event of cash flow problems until the money came in. It was very clear this was not a grant, and in accepting it Chapter still had to take the very real risk that the Appeal would not reach its agreed total, and they could be left with a debt to repay in future years. In the event only a small part of the underwriting offered was needed to help with cash flow during the reordering works, and all of that was repaid by the time the Project came to its conclusion.

We sent out our tender package as soon as possible to seven firms who had expressed provisional interest, and we were happy with. High profile as our Project was, only three responded: perhaps this was due to the tight timeline, combined with a recent upsurge in the building industry. Interviews took place in June and by 3 July we were in a pre-start meeting with the successful bidder, a firm called Fairhurst Ward Abbott Conservation (FWA), with offices in Huntingdon and Lichfield. Both David and I went off on our summer holidays the following week, returning in time for the agreed start on site of 5 August – the day after special services marking the outbreak of the First World War 100 years earlier. We agreed on a completion date of 31 January – giving us just seven short weeks between then and the reinterment itself to get everything else completed, rehearse the services and be ready to go. It was tight but I knew it was possible – indeed, it had to be. There was simply no alternative!

What we had to do was far from simple. To create the new ambulatory, as the right setting for the tomb, we needed to take down three of the large wooden screens Sir Charles Nicholson had erected in 1927, take them away into temperature-and-humidity-controlled storage until we could reinstate them in their new locations, remove all the wooden seating behind them, remove the old cathedra to the back of the cathedral pending its reinstatement in a side aisle;[23] take up the entire floor between the tower and the far east end of the cathedral; dig down to make preparation for new floors – as well as creating the vault to receive the coffin of the king; then put in the new floors in three different areas, as well as replacing heating and various electrical installations on the way. We were also taking the chance to completely renew the cathedral's old and erratic PA system as part of the work. And do all of this whilst maintaining the building as a working cathedral.

The first thing to do, therefore, was to 'seal off' the working area with floor to ceiling screens. The main way into Leicester Cathedral is the south door, and we gave over the smaller north door as a contractors' entrance. This meant about half of the cathedral, from the area under the tower eastwards, became a building site, out of bounds to visitors and staff alike, leaving us with the west end for all services and events. The large hoardings inside presented us with a problem – and an opportunity. The congregation would be facing straight at them every service for six months: what should we be looking at? In the end we settled for an ingenious solution, suggested by a member of our FAC, Paul Moore, who was the technical director of Curve, our local theatre. We had high-resolution photos of the view of the old screen and furnishings taken from the west end, had them blown up into the right size and fixed them to the screen. To all intents and purposes what you saw from August to January would be what you'd always seen. Only when it came down at the end was the transformation visible! There were also a couple of 'windows' put into the side hoardings, to enable the public to see the work as it went on.

---

23 There had been quite a debate with CFCE and the heritage bodies about the logic of keeping the old cathedra in the building when we wanted to commission a new one, as a bishop can clearly only have one official seat making the church a cathedral. In the end we agreed to keep the old one as an interesting piece of furniture of its time – but to be very clear that the new seat would be the 'real' one.

The photograph of the Nicholson screen, placed exactly
where it had stood for 87 years. It was later replaced, one
archway further east.

As all good Ricardians know, 22 August was the date in
1485 on which Richard III died at Bosworth. The ledger stone
in the choir area marking his burial "in this parish" had been
the focus of memorial services and events on or near that date
for over 30 years, ever since it was put in place, but this year the
service had to be held further west, in the part of the cathedral
left to us. By pure coincidence, 22 August was the day the
contractors were ready to lift that stone from its place in the
floor. It took nine men to lift it, and it was then securely stored
on site, pending a decision on its ultimate fate.[24]

The Church of St Martin has stood on the site for at least
900 years, and for much of that time people would have been
buried within its walls, as well as around it. Some of those
burials we knew about, but record keeping down the centuries
has been erratic at best and most were unknown. We also knew

---

24   There was some debate as to what would happen to the ledger stone, which
belongs to the cathedral, but clearly its function was about to be overtaken by the
tomb itself. In the end it was agreed to place it on extended loan in the new King
Richard III Visitor Centre over the road.

*Close-up of the top of Rachel Walker's coffin, one
of several uncovered during the works. The dates
are just visible.*

the Victorians had already dug up the floor and replaced it in
the last great alterations in the 1860s. So we weren't quite sure
what we'd find as we dug down. In the event, quite soon we
began to find a significant amount of what the archaeologists
call 'disarticulated remains' – old bones to you and me. We'd
agreed to do one of two things if such remains were found:
either we'd work around them disturbing as little as possible,
or else if they had to be removed they would be kept on site
(that is, within consecrated ground) before being reburied
when the project reached an appropriate phase. So it was
that we began to accumulate what eventually amounted to 13
boxes of such remains, kept to one side in the vestry. It was
a different matter, however, when in the chancel area (nearest

the high altar) a complete burial vault was found and within it a coffin clearly marked, "Rachel Walker Died 5th April 1847". We could find no other record of this burial, although there are wall memorials to a Sir William Walker, Mayor of Leicester in 1814 and High Sheriff of Leicestershire in 1823 who died in 1825, and to two other members of his family. In accordance with agreed protocol, the grave space was filled with pea gravel and covered with a sheet of plywood, ready to be bridged over with concrete slabs the next day. Come the next day, however, both coffin and pea gravel had apparently disappeared! It turned out that, far from being the only coffin in there, what we had found was only the top layer of a much deeper burial vault, presumably full of other Walkers. In the night the weight of the gravel had broken through the decayed wooden floor of the top layer of the vault, and Rachel had gone to join her wider family.[25] We didn't investigate further – this was a building project, not an archaeological dig – but simply bridged over what was there and made it secure, ready for the new floor in due course. This was in fact one of two burial vaults uncovered, along with eight brick-lined graves, some with identifiable individuals in. The most prominent of these was Agnes Vaughan, second wife of the 19th-century vicar,[26] whose three sons had also followed him in a veritable clergy dynasty. She had been buried right under the high altar, where her husband and sons had celebrated countless services over the decades. Unfortunately the reduced floor level meant she could not be replaced *in situ*, but her coffin and remains were moved a few metres to join the Walkers in their larger and deeper family vault.

---

25   Diligent research by Irene Turlington, our voluntary historian, revealed that Rachel was, in fact, the daughter-in-law of Sir William Walker, and had lived nearby in St Martin's parish.
26   Her coffin plate reads: "Agnes Vaughan Born May 24 1786 Died December 28 1878".

Eventually, of course, all the remains not covered over where they lay had to be reburied. So it was that, one morning in early January 2015, I found myself presiding over a reinterment of a slightly different style and nature to that which was to follow eight weeks later. Thirteen boxes of human remains were emptied into a deep space created for the purpose, and I said over them suitable prayers from the burial service adapted to the occasion, before they were covered back over, with a congregation made up of a verger and several builders. The service was utterly contrasting in style to that which was to follow for Richard: the theology and intent exactly the same, committing remains back to the earth and commending to God's merciful keeping those who had died many years before, "in sure and certain hope of the resurrection of the dead".

As the work proceeded over the months we kept track through monthly formal progress meetings, weekly visits from Yuli Lee, the member of Josh's staff overseeing this part of the Project, and almost daily contact between myself, Rob Pell, the site foreman, and Peter Collett, our Head Verger, who held formal responsibility for the cathedral building. By early autumn, FWA had managed to secure as site office rooms in a vacant building on the street corner opposite the cathedral,[27] so most of our meetings were held in an upstairs room there. There were often coffee and doughnuts, and a certain amount of intense conversation as Josh revealed a tough side to his apparently gentle nature, but on the whole what went on in the site meeting stays in the site meeting. Suffice it to say that by the end of January we knew we were finishing the work on time, and on budget. Which was just as well given everything else we still had to do!

---

27   In fact the contractors for Cathedral Gardens, Caseys, also had their site office there from November 2013 to the end of 2014 when they finally finished their work – and we were later able to secure rooms there for our floral team to work out of during the reinterment week itself. It turned out to be a very useful building – so much so that it is now in diocesan ownership!

Inside the hoardings, looking west. The vault for Richard
III's grave can be seen in the foreground.

What was unveiled as the hoardings came down was the
east end of the cathedral fundamentally reordered, not just to
provide for the tomb of a king but to do so in a way that placed
that in the right context within the whole building, and the
life of those who worship there. Beneath the central tower, at
the heart of the cathedral, is the new sanctuary, with a place
for a new, central altar-table. Open on three sides, the new
floor consists of a series of large circles of black marble, set
in much paler stone. At the back is the large, gilded wooden
screen created by Sir Charles Nicholson, now reconstructed
in its new location one bay further east than before. Behind
the screen lies the new space of the ambulatory,[28] in the midst
of which, at this stage, was the brick-lined vault, ready to
receive the coffin. The floor around this was also new, a series
of squares of Ancaster red sandstone, with white roses carved

---

28 Literally a 'walking place', formerly used for a place set aside in a monastery
for the monks to walk and reflect, but in this context a place to walk around the
tomb.

into four of the intersections to form a larger square around the tomb. To the north and south were two of Nicholson's wooden screens, which had not been altered in any way, with doorways which would from now on form the main ways into and out of the ambulatory, via the existing Chapels of St Dunstan and St Katharine. Beyond that again, at the very east end of the church, the former sanctuary was reshaped into a new Chapel of Christ the King. Where the altar rails had stood, two of Nicholson's side screens had been altered to form a new divider between the ambulatory and the chapel, which itself had eight canons' stalls at its west end (attached to the screens), and the altar rails moved further east to create a new, much smaller sanctuary occupied by what had formerly served as the high altar. The floor here now mirrors the intricate patterns put in by the Victorian architect Raphael Brandon in his 1860s' reordering, taken up from the spaces forming the new sanctuary and ambulatory.

So the space for the tomb of the earthly king, itself neither a chapel nor a shrine, lies bounded by chapels where the church's worship continues daily, in a pattern familiar to Richard's own medieval times, and in the shadow of the great east window depicting the heavenly King, Christ coming in glory at the last.

The windows and the pall

There were two other significant items we wanted to mark the reinterment that also needed getting right. The first was a pair of two commemorative windows, to go in St Katharine's Chapel, next to the ambulatory. The second was a pall, or burial cloth, to place over the coffin whilst it lay in the cathedral.

As a fixture, the windows also needed the consent of CFCE. We talked to Tom Denny, one of the foremost makers of stained glass working in England today, about designs, and put them forward to CFCE as a separate item, alongside the wider reordering, and approval was given in March, at the same time as the wider scheme. Tom's art has a lot of detail, which repays close and careful study, and his designs cleverly brought together aspects of Richard's life and story with that of common human experience. We were convinced this would add significantly to the beauty and ambience of the place of reinterment. However, the windows were due to cost us around £75,000 and so had to be seen as the final call on our fundraising, after the main work was secure. In the event we were only able to give Tom the final go-ahead to proceed shortly before reinterment. It takes up to 12 months for such delicate and detailed work to be completed, so the windows could only be installed in St Katharine's shortly after Easter 2016 – where they add yet more to the visitor's experience of the place of reinterment.

The pall, however, clearly had to be ready for the reinterment events. We worked with leading textile designer Jacquie Binns, giving her a free hand to interpret our broad requirements, and after discussing a few versions settled on a design which is on black velvet and incorporates on one side a series of figures portraying the people involved in the event itself, and on the other side medieval equivalents.[29] These are complemented by images of seraphim, and on top a place for the replica crown, which had been commissioned by the historian and member of the Looking for Richard team, John Ashdown-Hill, and donated to the cathedral to go with Richard's reinterment. The pall didn't need CFCE approval, only that of FAC and Chapter, which it duly got, and the cost,

---

29 The contemporary figures are: to the left, from the university Sir Bob Burgess (Vice Chancellor), Richard Buckley and Jo Appleby; to the right, from the Looking for Richard team Phil Stone, Philippa Langley and John Ashdown-Hill; and in the centre a group of City Mayor, Sir Peter Soulsby, Bishop Tim and Dean David.

some £8,000, was met by part of a grant we received from the Heritage Lottery Fund to help us 'tell the story' better. Jacquie came up to us several times, and I also visited her at her home and workshop in west London, to see work progressing. She completed work on the pall by the end of January 2015, and she and her husband brought it up in their car on 14 March, just two weeks before it was needed. It then spent a while on top of the cupboard in our team office, which strangely enough also contained several other vital items, such as the crown. The pall remains on permanent display in the cathedral, and attracts almost as much interest as the tomb itself.

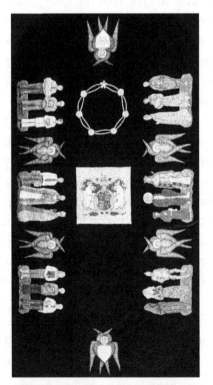

The pall created by Jacquie Binns laid out flat so all the images are clearly visible.

CHAPTER SEVEN

FINAL PREPARATIONS

Early Spring 2015

As outlined above, the design of the tomb itself had attracted much controversy but was finally settled when CFCE approved the plans in March 2014. However, its construction was quite another matter – deliberately kept separate from the main contract for alterations to the building. In addition the new sanctuary required a new altar-table[30] as well as seating for the clergy and others leading services. The design also specified a new cathedra, and the removal of the fixed canons' seats meant it was appropriate to provide new seating for more formal occasions. In addition the choir had regularly made use of the canons' seats in Nicholson's 'Chapter House'[31] and new choir stalls were also desirable. This was not only quite a shopping list, but also these items needed to be individually able to stand the test of time in the cathedral and ideally show some sense of fitting together as recognisably part of the same 'family' of

---

30   Some parts of the Church of England regularly say 'altar' whilst others, echoing the more Protestant origins of the church, prefer the name 'table'. A cathedral needs to serve the church in all its breadth, and so we opted to use the combined word. The eventually approved design also reflects both theological elements.

31   So much so that the seating within the Chapter House area was regularly referred to simply as 'the choir stalls'.

work done at this time. And all of this work also had to be ready for the date of the reinterment.

We had already decided on the materials for the tomb – wanting them as far as possible all to be sourced within the British Isles. The large tombstone on top was to be of Swaledale fossil stone, not only coming from Yorkshire and so bearing testimony to the significant spell of Richard's adult life spent as 'lord of the north', but in itself visibly speaking of the passages of time and eternity, as the numerous trilobites captured in it bear testimony. The base was to be black Kilkenny marble. David Monteith often said that was to ensure it also had the Irish touch – but the truth is it presented the best colour contrast to be found in the British Isles.

The search was now on for someone with the skills and knowledge to create the tomb we had designed. Back in the summer of 2014, as work in the cathedral got under way, Josh had been looking around for where to source the stone we needed. He was working with a firm called Britannicus, who specialised in procuring British stone. Their MD, Orlando Boyne, said he knew just the man we needed, and as Josh asked around a little more, the same name kept coming up. His name was James Elliott, and as luck would have it he had not long since relocated his business to the small Rutland town of Market Overton – just 30 or so miles from Leicester. So James it was who was given the job of taking these tomb designs from paper and hard drive and turning them into an actual honest-to-goodness tomb. James is an amazing character, whom Josh and I got to know pretty well in the intense months from summer 2014 to March 2015. He's well over 6 foot tall, disconcertingly direct in his approach, and basically he either takes to you or he doesn't. If he does – there's nothing he won't do to make things work. If not – well, probably he'll find a reason to focus on another job. James understands his material from the inside out: he's a craftsman of the old school. But he also applies modern technology. His design computer is one of the most powerful you can get; he probably knows more about fixing faults and the use of resins than anyone living – and he packs a 3D printer into his workshop, which he uses to create all the essential items to make things work that you just can't get 'off the shelf'. Stone, James told me, is not just stone. It has a grain, like wood. The reason so many masons don't succeed in their work is they don't know how to treat the material with respect, even love. And when he turns the massive blocks with his lifting gear, he can hear the stone speaking to him.

In September Josh, James and I visited Orlando at a stone works in Cumbria to select the block of Swaledale stone we would use to create the tomb. Orlando had several ready for us to look at, quarried in Yorkshire but transported there for storage and preparation prior to sale. It was James and Josh's advice that meant we took the smaller of two blocks put before us – because the fossils lay in the right direction, even though

James Elliott (mason), Josh McCosh (lead designer) and Pete Hobson in Cumbria with the just-chosen piece of swaledale fossil stone.

the dimensions were very tight. But James could see the result in the unfinished block in front of us – and that's the one we chose. The story of how that block was transported back to Rutland, then sliced and carved to tolerances of fractions of a millimetre, before the deeply incised cross was cut into it, and then the whole polished until it shone is a saga in itself. Fortunately James had it all filmed by a young film-maker, Alex J. Wright, and a visual telling of the whole story is now available online on his website.

As well as the block on top there was the not so small matter of the plinth to make. Far from being one big block with a hole cut in the middle (as some of us initially but naively imagined), it was made up of a large number of pieces, designed individually on James' computer and turned out in his workshop, designed to be able to bear the load of some 2.3 tonnes of tombstone – not just for a year or a decade, but in perpetuity. The side and end faces had also been carefully engraved in the Market Overton workshop by stone-cutter Gary Breeze, with Richard's name, dates and motto, and four carved boars, his personal insignia. Gary also carved the stone roses on the floor. All of this was done to a timetable to be ready by the end of January, because it then had to be installed well before reinterment. The plinth was put together on site in a manner resembling nothing so much as a very high-tech work of furniture assembly – and it took the best part of February to complete to James' satisfaction. The final touch was the *pietra dura* coat of arms, every piece of which was made from polished coloured stone by craftsman Thomas Greenaway.[32] This was carefully lowered into place once the main body of the plinth had been installed in the cathedral.

---

32 Working in *pietra dura* (literally 'hard stone') is a medieval craft, practised by very few today. Thomas is the only current practitioner in the UK, and he learned his trade from a family workshop in Italy. The coloured stones involved are duke's red from Devon, lapis lazuli from Afghanistan and yellow chalcedony from Italy.

Thomas Greenaway's pietradura coat of arms,
just after it had been placed into the plinth.

The wooden furnishings, meanwhile, had been through a separate process of design and commissioning, involving the Fabric Group, Chapter and the FAC, and were made by Luke Hughes & Company, one of the foremost designers of ecclesiastical furnishings in the country. These also had to be created and delivered in time to meet that window of February and early March.

The new altar-table and cathedra were larger matters. The cathedra was the subject of a design competition, with five submissions, the winner being chosen by Bishop Tim, David and Mandy, with Josh and myself in attendance. The winning artist was Francesco Draisci, whose design succeeded best in meeting the brief of being a seat that was at once lightweight enough to be movable, striking in appearance and yet visually anchored to the fabric. Francesco came up with a design which sits at rest on the north-east corner of the new sanctuary, with a large curved cross suspended above it. It's already proved itself one of those pieces of work you either love or hate – but on balance I think most will learn to love it. I certainly do!

But if all of that was running up against tight timelines, the altar-table was something else again! The earliest computer models of the new sanctuary had simply a cube shown in the centre. As the autumn drew on discussions developed on what exactly this should look like. A theological paper was presented to Chapter, outlining the varied considerations and how they might affect the finished product. We also had a series of meetings with a group from CFCE who were officially interested in the progress we were making on the reordering – but in practice were very interested in the fixtures and fittings, none more so than where the Eucharist or Lord's Supper is celebrated – in other words the place where daily and weekly we "Do this in remembrance of me". Josh prepared a series of images for us, and gradually the finished product emerged. A design was finally approved by Chapter in November for a table shape clad in alabaster, a beautiful material much used in past years for church and secular furnishings.[33] The problem was we needed quite a lot of it – more than existed above ground, and none had been mined in the UK since the 1950s. Once again, James came to the rescue. Alabaster is made of the same material as gypsum, and he and Orlando knew of a working mine in Fauld in Staffordshire where raw alabaster still existed, although it was no longer considered economic to mine it. James was sure we could extract enough from there – if only we could persuade them to let us. The argument was put – and won. We could have it, if we could get it out. So it was that during December James took a team thousands of feet below the surface of Staffordshire and several miles

---

33 It had been used in the Victorian restorations of the cathedral by Raphael Brandon, and more significantly, according to records, was the material used when in the summer of 1494 Henry VII belatedly ordered a tomb to be made for Richard in the Greyfriars. This tomb, however, never survived the demolition of Greyfriars in 1537, with the dissolution of the monasteries at the hands of his son, Henry VIII.

along passages, and eventually emerged victorious with a block just large enough for our purposes. He then sliced and carved this to form, secured it to a framework specially made for us by a firm of theatrical designers,[34] and the whole was delivered into the cathedral on Thursday 19 March – just in time for specialists to put the gilding on the metal edges linking the alabaster faces. It was there in time – but only just.[35] And the week itself began with a moving service on Saturday evening 21 March, when Bishop Tim dedicated the new altar-table, and the coming week ahead, in the presence of a small congregation made up almost entirely of cathedral and diocesan staff. For us, it was the perfect way to prepare for the days ahead.

Preparing for the services

So much for getting the cathedral ready for reinterment. But what would people be coming to? We had had two years to think this through, and as it turned out it was needed, because really we were about to do something no one had done before, that is, 530 years after their first burial to reinter the remains of an anointed king of England. You just don't take the services for that off the shelf!

As our 'Narrative for the Week' had developed, it had become clear what we needed was not just one but in fact three services. One to receive the coffin and remains into the cathedral; a second for the reinterment itself, with in-between a period of time when we thought people might like to view the coffin 'lying

---

34 It amused us that their name is 'Clockwork Scenery', and their MD was a Mr George Orange. They became known informally in the office as 'the Clockwork Orange people'!

35 There was a 'Plan B' to use painted hardboard in place of the alabaster for the reinterment week, and finish it all off properly afterwards. None of us wanted to do that – and in the event we didn't need to. But James later told us he was working 20-hour days at the end to get it all finished.

in repose'.[36] And given the design of the tomb, a third, once the massive tombstone with the incised cross had been put in place overnight, to mark the completion of the whole event.

Alongside the question of what words and music to use, a much wider issue raised its head. Leicester Cathedral is a Church of England cathedral, but wasn't King Richard a Catholic? He lived and died in the period a generation or two before the English Reformation, which led to the creation of the Church of England – famously to suit the political and marital needs of Henry VIII, the son of Henry Tudor whose defeat of Richard at Bosworth brought the Tudor dynasty into power.[37] Ever since that time the Church of England has been the established church of the nation and every monarch has been crowned as such by the Archbishop of Canterbury of the day, up to and including Queen Elizabeth II. So should the reinterment services be Catholic or Protestant? As with so many such questions, the preferred answer depends, to a large degree, on who's asking. By 'catholic' many really meant 'Roman Catholic', that is, the church that looks to the Pope, the Bishop of Rome, as its earthly leader. But 'catholic' strictly speaking means simply 'worldwide' – and the claim of the Church of England at the Reformation and since is that it is indeed the proper successor to the English church of Richard's day, the catholic church of the land. St Martin's Church in that

---

36 Some people wanted us to use the phrase 'lying in state' for this period, but it was made very clear to us from the Palace that this only applies if the monarch so rules. In the absence of such direction we were very happy to adopt the phrase 'lying in repose', as equally descriptive. This was far from the only instance where different expectations of the event led to disappointment in various circles.

37 It has even been suggested that had Richard won at Bosworth there would have been no English Reformation, and no Church of England as we know it. This is of course mere speculation, but the roots of the Reformation across Europe were far wider than Henry VIII's political desires. Indeed, what we know of Richard suggests he might have been very sympathetic to many of them – for example, the use of English for the language of worship and the Bible.

sense was catholic in Richard's time and is still catholic today.[38] In any case, it had been legally established that reinterment was to happen in Leicester Cathedral, and it would not have been possible in church law for us to have a Roman Catholic service there. But we could, of course, work closely with our Roman Catholic colleagues – and we did, from the word go.

Practical responsibility for services and music in a cathedral lies with the Canon Precentor, and so from early on a Liturgy Group had been formed, led by Johannes Arens, but incorporating a wide range of other expertise to look at the services needed. One such was the Oxford-based medieval scholar Dr Alexandra Buckle, who had not long before unearthed copies of an old manuscript containing a full medieval rite used for the reinterment of remains – not indeed for a monarch but for an Earl of Warwick. It was even possible something of this nature had been used when in 1476 Richard's brother, King Edward IV, had arranged the reinterment of their father and brother from Pontefract to their family home at Fotheringhay with great ceremony. The Group was able to draw significantly from that source for the reinterment service itself, which would clearly be the national, and indeed international, showpiece of the week.

The first service of the week was to be called the 'Reception of Remains', and it was decided early on to base this on the service of Compline, a service that was in regular use in the medieval church and is still used widely today in both Catholic and Anglican churches, as well as others. It is the service used to mark the close of the day, and was very appropriate for a day that would begin with the coffin leaving the university, and

---

38 The very title 'Roman Catholic' only came into use in the 16th century and was not in widespread use until much later than that. It would not have been known at all in Richard's day.

would end with its reception into the cathedral with prayer. This would also mark the cathedral, as a Christian community, receiving the coffin of the former monarch.

That left the third service, when the tomb would be revealed. We were initially unclear what to call this. Should it be 'Celebration', to mark a week's work done? But was that quite the right word to sum up the mood? We weren't sure. In the end we recognised that this would be the first time the tomb in all its glory would be seen – and so it became the 'Service of Reveal'. We did, however, feel that by this stage of the week this service would provide a particular focus for Leicester and Leicestershire to mark what had been done in their midst, and would stay there. We therefore agreed to invite Curve, Leicester's own theatre, to work with us in the creation of this service. As it happens Nikolai Foster was due to take up his post as new artistic director at Curve in January 2015, and this challenge for him at the very start of his time in the city was one to which he rose with enthusiasm.

Keith Cousins, holding a copy of the Reinterment service book for 26th March – one of a set of three, including the Compline on 22nd and the Reveal on 27th.

The music would obviously also be central to the services. We were very clear we wanted to provide this ourselves, rather than bring in numbers of external musicians, and so it fell to Dr Chris Ouvry-Johns, as the cathedral's Director of Music, to advise the Group and to preside over the delivery of what was agreed.

So the services gradually came together – a mixture of the medieval and the modern, the existing and the newly written. We wanted some significant new pieces to have a place: for the reinterment service we commissioned the Poet Laureate, Carol Ann Duffy, to write a piece, the composer Judith Bingham to write an anthem[39] and Judith Weir, Master of the Queen's Music, to create a new setting for the National Anthem. Carol Ann Duffy's poem, titled simply 'Richard',[40] was read in the reinterment service by the noted actor Benedict Cumberbatch, who was himself due to appear in a televised version of the story of Richard III the following year. Such is the pressure on the lives of media celebrities that he could only turn up on the morning of the service itself, and there was no time for him to rehearse in the cathedral. So at the two final rehearsals, the afternoon before and that morning, I stood in for him. I still maintain my reading was at least as good as his later on in the day.

There was a lot of pressure on us to release the text of the services in advance. But we held firm and it was only as invited guests filed into the cathedral for the three services on the days that they found copies on their seats.

---

39   The anthem, 'Ghostly Grace', was based on a 13th-century text by the abbess St Mechtilde. Judith had been inspired by seeing in the British Library a copy of her *Book of Ghostly Grace* that Richard III had owned, with his signature and that of his wife, Anne, on it.
40   The full text of the poem was also kept a closely guarded secret until the service itself, but is now freely available, and is reproduced in full at the front of this book.

Who should attend?

Apart from the texts and music there was the equally difficult matter of who should be invited to be present for the services. Leicester is not a large cathedral, and we reckoned to fit in only around 600 guests to each service, once the musicians and leading clergy were allowed for. That was a total of 1,800 people at most who could attend any one of the three services. How would they be chosen? This above all was a matter on which we were inundated with letters, emails and phone calls. So many people had what was, in their eyes, an absolutely cast-iron reason why they, above all, should be invited. And then there was the question of all the 'usual suspects' who expect to be invited to big events at a cathedral.

We were clear that as this was an invitation to the cathedral service, it should ultimately be issued in the name of the Dean, who is responsible for the cathedral. The handling of the practical managing of invitation lists was given to the 'Civic and Ceremonial' Workstream, which I sat on, but the overall direction was set by the cathedral – and fully endorsed by our partner organisations. We were also clear that if this was to be an event witnessing to the hope Christian faith has to say to all of us in the face of death, then it should be in principle possible for anyone to attend. But there was no way we could simply open the doors on a first-come first-served basis until we were full, like a January sale – so we came up with the public ballot. There were, of course, certain people we would definitely want to invite – but it was agreed that one place in three at each service would be open to the general public, simply on the basis of application and random selection. So between 12 and 31 December 2014 people were invited to apply online, or by post if necessary, for the chance to receive one of 200 invitations to each one of the services – so 600 places in all. The only other constraint on the process was for half of these places to be for local people (Leicester and Leicestershire) and half for the 'rest of the world'. We didn't know how many would take us up on this, and were amazed when by the closing date around 14,500 people had applied, from 19 countries all around the globe – including names from Japan, Afghanistan and the Democratic Republic of the Congo. We had promised a random draw, and to do that we used a random sequence generator based on atmospheric noise – apparently amongst the most random sources available to us on the planet! I well remember the first day back after New Year when Keith Cousins, Emma Wigley and myself sat down at a computer with all 14,000 listed, and then randomised their order, effectively picking the first 600 as those who would receive invitations. The randomising itself took a few seconds: accurately reading off the names, checking which services they'd asked to be considered for, and making sure they hadn't improperly submitted more than one application,[41] took us the best part of two days! And just to show what 'random' throws up, no one was more surprised than I when we read off the first name coming up on the list – and it turned out to be none other than a good friend of mine, who I hadn't even known had applied. But then the million-to-one chance of finding the 'king in the car park' in the first place had inured us to lesser coincidences!

The whole exercise attracted quite a bit of publicity, not only locally but also nationally and internationally. People got very excited about the 'golden ticket' idea – and yes, we were aware of the similarities with Willie Wonka and his Chocolate Factory – though we did repeatedly have to explain that what was available was not in fact a 'ticket' that might be bought or sold on or exchanged with a friend, but a personalised invitation

---

41   We were rigorous on this, checking not only names and addresses and emails used, but also the IP number it came from and is reproduced in full at the front of this book.

from the Dean to a service in the cathedral. When we announced
the results I was asked to deliver two of the first local ones 'out
of the hat' in person, so it was that I delivered one invitation
live on local Breakfast TV to one delighted fan, and another by
phone call live on local radio to a woman, who was invited to
the cathedral later that morning to receive it. Both turned out
to be lifelong Ricardian fans, and their reactions were suitably
gratifying!

Apart from the matter of the general public, there was the
question of who should make up the rest of the congregation.
To help us share round the limited number of places as widely as
possible, alongside the public ballot we had agreed two further
underlying principles. Firstly, unless there was a particular
reason, no one should expect to receive an invitation to more
than one service; and, secondly, with very few exceptions, invites
went only to individuals, not to 'plus ones'. This, interestingly,
was the single issue that created more trouble than any other, as
so many people apparently expected to 'bring their partner' as
of right – but we held firm.

The nature of the services as we had prepared them helped us
a bit here. So the Reception service was focussed on the cathedral
itself. As well as its own core clergy and regular congregation,
every cathedral has a wider circle of people actively involved in
its life – the Cathedral Chapter, the College of Canons and the
Cathedral Council are all formal bodies prescribed by church
(and so state) legislation. We needed to make sure they were
invited. Then there were the parishes of the diocese, some 300
of them – they needed to know they were included, at least to
some degree, and this was the service to do that. The Reveal
service was a more local celebration, and we wanted a strong
element of young people present there, as well as other local
community groups – and Leicester is a city full of many and
diverse communities.

The Reinterment was the centrepiece, and the guest list needed to include all sorts of people, not least a national element. And here, from the beginning, one question had regularly been put to us: "Is the Queen going to be there?" We understood the interest, and there was, of course, a fair case for the reigning monarch to be present at the reinterment of one of her predecessors, however mired in the mists of time his own accession to that throne might have been. But this was never a matter for us to decide. All we could do was talk through the 'usual channels' and await the outcome. I'm convinced the fuss attending the Judicial Review didn't help here as the royal family are very concerned to avoid matters that might be deemed controversial. But even after that was settled, the matter of royal attendance took a long while to resolve. The Queen's cousin, the current Richard, Duke of Gloucester, was our Appeal Patron, and we obviously wanted him to attend. Eventually all was made clear: as well as both the Duke and Duchess of Gloucester coming to the Reinterment, Sophie, Countess of Wessex would attend as the most senior royal – and that explicitly on behalf of the Queen. We were happy with the result – if a little frustrated by the time it had taken to be arrived at.

Alongside royal representation, our local MPs and members of the House of Lords and representatives of national bodies required inclusion. Key people from the Looking for Richard team, the university dig team and the Richard III Society needed to be there, and our TV partners wanted a sprinkling of names and celebrities who could also appear in their studio discussions. We were clear that we wanted to invite all of the 'Bosworth Peers', representing the bringing together of the Houses of York and Lancaster. This was also the service where major donors to the Appeal might properly expect an invitation (we defined 'major donor' as those who had given at least £10,000). It was not an easy task – but in the end it was settled.

The actual sending out of invitations and then, once people had replied (because not everybody, in the end, was able or even wanted to accept), of actual Admission Cards and the checking of IDs for security purposes, was a massive exercise, which I'm glad to say was carried out by a team masterminded heroically by Tim Webster, of the county council, who led that Workstream. The allocation of seats, also a potential nightmare as everybody of course wanted the 'best seats' in a building where wherever you sat you would only see a part of the 'action', was shared between Tim's team and a team at the cathedral led by me.

The floral team

Over the decades white roses had periodically appeared in the cathedral on and around the ledger stone, notably around 22 August each year, and the white rose was clearly going to be central to events – many thousands were in evidence during the week itself. But that was, of course, just the tip of the iceberg florally speaking. We needed a team who could decorate the cathedral appropriately, and respond to the many other needs for supplying flowers during the week, and managing those brought and left in abundance by others. Since this was a far bigger exercise than the cathedral's voluntary flower arrangers could be expected to take on, we were very fortunate to be able to invite Rosemary Hughes to take on leadership of this task. Rosie is a professional florist, and also the daughter-in-law of a former canon of the cathedral, who still lives locally. She is also Supplier of Nosegays by Appointment to the Queen. From October 2014 we were meeting with Rosemary making our plans, and she in turn brought together a team of seven who between them kept the cathedral in order, florally speaking. This involved very long days during the reinterment week, as arrangements had to be tended to early in the mornings, before the cathedral opened to visitors, and late at night after it closed. Her guiding principle was to use only English plants that would have been known in Richard's day[42] – extended to the fact that the main displays were all mounted in hollowed-out tree stumps as would have been medieval practice. Alongside the white rose, the broom plant also featured heavily as might be expected,[43] and on the Wednesday 25 March lilies, traditional for what in the church's year is Lady Day – the feast of the Annunciation to the Virgin Mary. The floral team's base opposite the cathedral was a hub positively buzzing with activity and high spirits throughout the reinterment week.

Rehearsals

The final part of preparation was, of course, rehearsals, as indicated above. We had three quite different services, all wholly under wraps, the first two of which were to be televised live, and all involving a whole cast of people – both national figures and local cast. There was the small matter of the formal Reception of the coffin to be choreographed, involving a member of the royal family; there were sundry other processions of clergy, dignitaries and key people who had made up the story; there were words to be said and music to be played and sung. And for the Reveal service, an entire three-part dramatic dance to music from a team of local dancers recruited and rehearsed by Nikolai and his colleagues from Curve. And all of that in a cathedral which was only available in any sort of state to be used from mid-February. In the end it all worked surprisingly well. We had an intensive day of 'walk-and-talk-through' of all three services on 28 February, as well as a series of separate practice runs of key moments such as the arrival of the coffin at the cathedral

---

42   Mainly holly, yew, ivy, rosemary and willow, all locally sourced.
43   The Latin name *planta genista* gave its name to the Plantagenet dynasty, as its founding father, Geoffrey of Anjou, characteristically wore a sprig in his hat.

and the placing of the pall. We then had a final run-through
with the cameras 'as live' on the days before each of the actual
services themselves. Those were an interesting experience, as
leadership was shared at any given moment between Johannes
as Precentor, myself as Project Manager, Bridget Caldwell as
the Floor Manager in the building and Rachel Morgan as the
Executive Producer in the TV truck outside, talking to Bridget
on her headphones. Fortunately we managed to get everything
lined up as we all respectively wanted it. It was a bit different
for final rehearsals of the Reveal early on the Friday morning
(fortunately for us not transmitted live on TV[44]), after a most-
of-the-night session putting the tombstone in place on top.

With the aid of stand-ins for the Archbishop of Canterbury,
the Cardinal Archbishop of Westminster, the Duke of Gloucester
(twice) and Benedict Cumberbatch, all was completed and each
service was ready to go at the due time. So it was we arrived at
the week itself, ready to do what had never been done before,
and do it with dignity and honour – and before the eyes of
the world. But just how interested would the world be? That
remained to be seen.

Preparing the remains

The story of the research both to identify the remains as truly
those of Richard III and then to see what they could tell us
about him has been very well told by the university team
themselves, in the book *The Bones of a King*. Whilst we were
kept well informed of all developments, it was always clear
that those bones remained the responsibility of the university
right up until the moment they were handed over to us for
reburial. But since the reburial itself was for us to arrange,

---

44 Though the performances of the young and older people would have made
spectacular viewing if it had been, and it was also partly captured by regional TV
news crews, who were filming for broadcast later that day.

there was inevitably much liaison needed over how to make those arrangements. From our end this was handled mainly through the Fabric Group, who consulted carefully both on medieval burial practices and on scientific expectations about the preservation of remains – where we were being told what was needed was to return the bones to the ground as nearly as possible in the condition in which they'd emerged, uncontaminated by their journey in-between. The initial plan was to place the bones in a small lead ossuary (literally a 'bone box'), which was both sympathetic to medieval practice and also gave the best chance of keeping the remains sterile, but to place that into an oak coffin – and we had decided early on to ask Michael Ibsen, whose DNA had helped confirm the identity of the king, to make that, which he'd willingly agreed to do. This plan, however, did not at all commend itself to Philippa Langley and her colleagues, whose own plan had provided for the bones to be laid out in anatomical order, stitched to purple cloth. They also wanted the coffining to be carried out in 'a place of sanctity', with prayers. And there were requests for various symbolic items to be placed in the coffin with the bones.[45]

Resolving the very different approaches to all of this took quite a bit of behind-the-scenes negotiation before we could reach a solution we could all agree on, or at least agree to

---

45 Philippa Langley is a very determined lady, and of course were she not then none of this would have been happening. She is also a good publicist and able to mobilise a significant number of others who shared her apparent scepticism about the cathedral's ability to make the right provisions for Richard III in quite a few aspects. I found myself over the months in dialogue with a number of these, notably a powerful trio of ladies who lived in different parts of the country, and only met through Twitter and a common desire to press us on such matters. As time went on we did, at my invitation, meet in person on a number of occasions, and whilst having to agree to differ on some matters, that definitely helped me understand the depth of feeling the last Plantagenet king arouses. I also met them several times during the reinterment week itself, and am pleased to say they expressed themselves very happy with the end result of all our planning!

differ on. I well remember a conversation with Philippa on this point on the steps of the Royal Courts of Justice, snatched in-between media interviews following the first abortive hearing on Judicial Review, where I assured her that this was one area where compromise might prove possible. As indeed turned out to be the case.

What was finally decided was that the bones would be in a lead ossuary, but that this would be large enough for them to be laid out 'in anatomical order', and so in effect what we would create would be a lead-lined coffin with a head-end and a foot-end,[46] in which the bones would be placed in order. They would not be stitched to a cloth – an idea fraught with difficulty, not least because of the sheer number and size of bones in a human skeleton – but would be held firmly in place by woollen packing, to prevent movement during the journeys we knew the coffin would need to take. There would be a plain linen cloth on top, which was embroidered by Elizabeth Nokes of the Richard III Society, and all of this would be sealed into the lead container, which would then be soldered shut. One item – a rosary – would be allowed to be placed into the coffin, above the wool but below the lid of the lead lining. This all sounded right in principle, but would it actually work? We arranged a day at the university with Richard Buckley and colleagues, when we placed a plastic skeleton into a large cardboard box, packed with loft insulation material, and then carried it around the Archaeology building, up and down stairs, and examined the outcome. It was all slightly surreal,

---

46 Strictly speaking a 'leg-end', as the feet were the only part missing from the skeleton when exhumed – presumed destroyed by Victorian building activity in the area, which had come close to making the whole search for Richard's remains fruitless. Presumably in that case many would have gone on repeating as 'historical fact' the story of their being dug up and thrown in the River Soar at the time of the Reformation. This idea had in fact been discredited in print as far back as 1920 and then several times thereafter. Local historian David Baldwin had written a significant paper about it in 1986, and this was reported in *The Times* in 1993.

but it definitely worked! The artificial remains were as safe in their place at the end as when we had started.

The precise location of the bones had been carefully shrouded in secrecy by the university, as were the actual arrangements for placing them into their coffined state. This was, however, another area where the Looking for Richard team had been very clear in their expectations that the remains should be coffined in 'a place of sanctity, with prayers'. We felt that this owed much to romantic imagination, but little or nothing to either historic precedent or contemporary funeral practice, as in neither case is there any pattern of prayers being said whilst the essentially practical task of placing remains in a box is carried out. The university team agreed with us on this – being keen themselves to distinguish the essentially scientific phase of the project from its more social and religious aspect.

The coffining itself therefore took place a week before the actual reinterment, in front of a carefully selected group of about 20 people who had been part of the story, which included the Anglican and Roman Catholic chaplains to the university, and also myself, on behalf of the cathedral. But we were all clearly there as observers, not as those taking part in the action. There was also an independent academic observer, from the University of York as it happened. We all signed a statement at the end confirming that we had witnessed every bone and fragment being placed into the coffin – which we had, but since we had also all been required to sign a non-disclosure agreement not to talk about the detail of what we saw, that's all I can report. But I can assure you that it did all go ahead as planned, and in a quiet and reverential, but clearly non-religious manner. I was there.

However, the concept of the coffined remains being kept for a period in an atmosphere of prayer and a place of sanctity before their final reburial was quite another matter. What could be a better 'place of sanctity' than our own cathedral? Where better to pray? This was to be something we would take very seriously in the period between their arrival in the cathedral and their eventual reinterment.

CHAPTER EIGHT

THE WEEK OF REINTERMENT

22-27 MARCH 2015

The week of the reinterment arrived. We knew what we wanted to do. We felt just about ready to do it. We also knew the ability of this story to stir strong feelings in many hearts and minds – but to be honest we still had no real idea how all that we had prepared would be received, or how many would come to be part of it. My worst nightmare was that we would have made all these preparations and only a few hundred people would turn up. But it was looking increasingly unlikely that was to be the case!

Towards the end of 2014 there was a lot going on in making ready for the reinterment, and Liz and her colleagues had been working hard to interest the national press in the stories – but found it quite hard going. There'd be a flurry of interest when anything 'controversial' emerged but beyond Leicester the positive stories we wanted to tell were falling on stony ground. But once the New Year turned, that began to change. It had been as early as summer 2013 that we'd reached agreement with Darlow Smithson Productions (DSP), the company who'd covered the original dig, that they and Channel 4 could have exclusive televised coverage of events inside the cathedral, but that still left a lot more coverage for everybody else.[47] We made it clear we'd issue accreditation to journalists for all sorts of background stories, access to the Gardens, and to put people into the building itself during services. The numbers applying started to build up, so that by the week itself we had representatives of over 200 different media organisations wanting to cover the story in one way or another, with over 950 journalists and technicians eventually in attendance from all over the world. Liz and her team had a lot to organise – and did it throughout with good humour and aplomb.

'Reception' – Sunday 22 March

Sunday morning dawned bright – and thankfully the day continued that way. It began with the coffined remains leaving the university and beginning the journey that would bring them to the Cathedral Gardens for precisely 5.45 pm that evening. The sun shone, and the crowds were out in their thousands to watch the final journey of this last Plantagenet king of England. We'd given thought in our preparations to the sort of atmosphere we might want to see for this day – always acknowledging that you can't tell people what to think and do! But we'd worked hard for the 'dignity and honour' theme to prevail – and so it did. White roses were there in abundance, many thrown at the cortège as it passed by. Any fears of demonstrations or inappropriate reactions were misplaced. The mood seemed to be a mixture of awe and wonder, and simple wanting to 'be there' – a theme that was to be repeated throughout the week that followed.

---

47   A lot of people asked us why not give coverage to the BBC. The simple answer is that when we asked them, back in 2013, if they were interested, the answer came back 'No'. Channel 4, however, who had covered the story through DSP from the very start, definitely were. We went with them, and didn't regret it. And we did ensure that the BBC gave extensive coverage from every area outside the cathedral itself.

The coffin containing the remains of Richard III leaves the University on 22nd March 2015, carried on the shoulders of staff from local funeral directors, A.J. Adkinson and Son.

Meanwhile, at the cathedral David was leading an early morning live service for Radio 4, which finished by 8.45 am. Our main Sunday morning congregation later joined with nearby St Mary de Castro for their 10.15 am service, but I and other key colleagues were gathering at the cathedral to begin a final run-through with cameras for that evening's service of Compline, for the Reception of the remains. Alongside our own final preparations, the whole previous week had been full of site crews bringing into the place all the paraphernalia that goes with live TV – most of which you never see on screen! By mid-afternoon we were rehearsed and ready to go. Those fortunate enough to have invitations to the service itself began arriving at the secure cordon around the cathedral soon after lunchtime, and having showed their invitations were admitted into Cathedral Gardens, and then from 4 pm into the cathedral itself – all to be seated by 5 pm. The checking of invitations and the appropriate seating of people inside was itself a complex task, which was overseen by the cathedral's usual volunteer team, supplemented by others.

Outside the crowds had been gathering from dawn, held back behind barriers on the opposite side of the street, so the Gardens were clear and ready to receive the cortège and coffin, and by 5 pm they were seven or eight deep and full of expectation. Some people had been at Bow Bridge at 4 pm where both City and Lord Mayors had gathered with 500 schoolchildren to greet the arrival of the cortège into the city, and had hurried over the 200 metres or so to see the final stage of the journey. Bishop Tim had accompanied the coffin on its long day's journey from university to cathedral via the site of Richard's death, the Bosworth Battlefield Visitor Centre and the villages significant in the story,[48] then into Leicester along the length of the A47. He too had parted company from the cortège at Bow Bridge and had hurried over to be ready to greet the remains at Cathedral Gardens with the Dean. The Duke of Gloucester had meanwhile arrived and been escorted into St Martins House next to the cathedral by a back door, and he and the representative Bosworth Peers were busy being briefed on their task of accompanying the coffin into the cathedral, and then placing the pall on top of it as the service began – a more complex task than you might think, given it would be done by them for the first time under the gaze of live TV cameras.[49]

Final TV interviews were concluded, and a mood of expectancy descended on the crowds outside and the cathedral

48   The smaller villages of Dadlington, where many of the battle slain were buried, and Sutton Cheyney, where tradition says Richard celebrated Mass the night beforehand, and then Market Bosworth itself, as the nearest community of any size, with battle memorials in its church.
49   Here, as elsewhere in our dealings with this group, we were deeply indebted to the invaluable work of Gordon and Janet Arthur, members of the cathedral congregation. Gordon, a recently retired solicitor, had just taken on the ceremonial role of High Sherriff, and he and Janet well understood that world.

within. The congregation had been seated by 5 pm and a series of processions had brought the cathedral and parish clergy into place by 5.30 pm. We had agreed the space in Cathedral Gardens between the road and the main entrance was to be clear for the final entrance – but although the complex series of movements and handovers that was to take place there had been rehearsed several times, I was the only person acquainted with it that wasn't needed to play a vital role within. So we'd agreed I would stand there, dressed in clerical robes and so not looking out of place, and act as unseen stage manager, just to be sure everybody remembered what to do and when. Hence suddenly, just after 5.30, I was left standing alone outside the cathedral, in the no man's land between the crowds opposite and the cathedral itself, awaiting the arrival of the cortège. I had an earpiece in and could hear Maggie Shutt, who was at the head of the procession, reporting to the Control Centre back in the Town Hall on where they were up to, and for a few long minutes it seemed as if time stood still. Everything I'd

The coffin arrives at the cathedral. The figure in white to the right of the entrance pillar is me

been working on for two and a half years was about to kick into action. The cathedral would now receive the remains of Richard III and lay them to rest in a tomb from which, as far as was in our power to ensure, they would never leave again. It was the moment of quiet at the eye of the storm.

The noise of the crowd rose; the voice in my ear told me they were turning the corner – and suddenly there they were, processing up Peacock Lane to the front of the cathedral itself. Both City and Lord Mayors and their consorts stepped forward and, led by the mace bearer, I escorted them into the cathedral – the final guests arriving before the coffin itself. The Bishop and Dean greeted them in the Vaughan porch at the cathedral's south door, then took up their position, halfway between the porch and the road. The Duke of Gloucester had already been escorted out of St Martins House by Lady Gretton, along with our four Bosworth Peers for the day,[50] and, after being presented to the Bishop and Dean, stood to one side, ready for his duties. Then came a moment of great significance: the formal handing over of the coffined remains of Richard III from the care of the University of Leicester into the custody of the cathedral for final reburial. We had discussed both when and how to do this many times in the Events and Exec Groups from early on and this had clearly been the right time and place. Richard Buckley, as the man issued with the licence for exhumation, stepped forward from behind the hearse, which he had also followed throughout the day,[51] and with a few well-chosen words placed the licence into the hands of the Dean, who accepted it, and with it the responsibility for all that was to follow. Richard walked on into the cathedral; the coffin was lowered from its horse-drawn

---

50   The Duke of Rutland and Hon. Thomas Orde-Powlett (House of York), and the Earl of Derby and Earl De La Warr (House of Lancaster).

51   Accompanied throughout by Canon Stephen Foster, the university's lead chaplain, and himself a former Precentor of the cathedral, and so representing the university's acknowledgement of the spiritual aspect of their charge.

The laying of the pall

gun carriage by six bearers. There was nothing more I could do, and as they walked slowly towards the Bishop and Dean I moved quickly into the cathedral and took my seat amongst my fellow clergy. Outside all was happening just as we had rehearsed it: as the coffin approached the Bishop and Dean they turned and led it into the cathedral; falling in behind were the four Bosworth Peers, united in this final journey, and last of all the Duke of Gloucester, occupying as it were the place both of chief mourner and of the current royal family as they brought towards their final rest the remains of one of their more controversial predecessors.

The service itself proceeded exactly as planned.[52] The placing of the pall went smoothly, and then on top of it a Bible dating from Richard's own time, loaned from the university's collection of ancient books, and the donated replica crown. We had debated how this should be done. I argued strongly that at this moment the impression given should be less of the majesty of

---

52 Copies of the full text of this, and the other two main services used in the week, have since been made available for those who want to study more fully. Details of how to obtain them are on the cathedral's website.

*Emma Chamberlain, chosen from amongst those
who successfully completed the new Richard III
Brownie badge, lays the crown on the coffin.*

a reigning monarch and more of the humanity of a slain man, and had concluded that it was an action best carried out by a young person. Emma Chamberlain, whose image has now been seen across the globe placing that crown, was a member of the 1ˢᵗ Aylestone Brownies, and was chosen as one of the first to successfully complete the new Brownie Richard III badge. The fact that our own Emma Wigley was her Brownie leader was, perhaps, not totally coincidental, and I felt proud of both of them as 'big Emma' accompanied 'little Emma' forwards, and then left her to place the crown on her own.

One of the ways we had resolved the vexed question of 'Catholic/Anglican' was to invite His Eminence Vincent Nicholls, Cardinal Archbishop of Westminster, and so the leading Roman Catholic bishop in the land, to be our honoured guest at the service and to preach the sermon. He did so with both eloquence and sensitivity, in that way making the point that at the most senior level our churches were united in doing this thing. He was also the next day to celebrate a Requiem Mass at Holy Cross Priory, our local Roman Catholic church, so ensuring that the full rites of that persuasion were also used with the highest authority.

At the end of the service, also the end of a long day for many, we had 600 people to see out, most of whom wanted to pass by the coffin itself, which they had not had the opportunity to see close up until that moment. But we also needed to set up for the following day's 'lying in repose', and meanwhile the TV crews needed to empty at least a significant part of their equipment out of the building, as it would not be needed for four more days. There was hospitality for the 200 or so guests we could cater for in St Martins House next door, and in the cathedral a flurry of activity as we rearranged the seating to be ready for the following day. We were under way. The reception that day gave hints of the incredible interest the rest of the week was to hold, as events captured the imagination of people not just locally but around the world.

'Lying in repose' – Monday to Wednesday 23-25 March

Monday also dawned bright, and as I drove in early for morning prayers, I wondered how many people would choose to come and file past the coffin, as the remains lay in repose. The queues were already there, but at that stage, just before 8 am, were perhaps only 100 strong – though some had been there since before 6 am. After prayers I led the quick daily briefing we had put in place for cathedral key staff, and then decided I'd do something I'd promised, which was to take the special floral arrangement that had lain on top of the coffin throughout its journey the previous day to the children of King Richard III

Infant School, about half a mile to the west. The naming of this school, located as it was very close to the route Richard took out to Bow Bridge in 1485, was just another indication that he had been, in a quiet but enduring way, part of Leicester's story for the past five centuries. The school had been one of the first to respond to our Community Challenge in the later stages of the Appeal, and the children had also been asked by Richard Buckley to sew linen bags that had gone into the coffin containing the smaller bones of the remains – hands and ribs, for example. I arrived on cue halfway through their morning assembly. They were delighted to see me and to receive the floral arrangement, and soon after I left to return to the cathedral. It was probably by then not quite 10 am. For speed, I'd gone in my car, which I normally parked behind the cathedral where there were one or two spaces. But as I approached I saw that the queue which only a couple of hours ago had been a hundred or so strong outside the front of the cathedral, had grown phenomenally, and now stretched right around the block, all along the back of the cathedral and St Martins House, and out into the new Jubilee Square. There was no way I could park where I usually did, so I headed off to the multi-storey nearby and walked back in on foot, to find the team in the cathedral bowled over by the demand to pass by the coffin. It was perhaps then, more even than the day before, that I realised just how important what we were doing was in the eyes of so many people, as they queued, for the most part good-naturedly, for hours in order to spend maybe two minutes inside the building filing past the coffin. We had to keep people moving, in order to allow as many as possible to have their turn – though we also arranged space for our visitors to light a candle, and to stay and say a prayer if they wanted to – which a good number did. We'd also put in place a team of chaplains to speak with people if they wanted to, reckoning that the cathedral clergy would be likely to be otherwise engaged most of the time. They too found demand overwhelming – both inside and increasingly outside. That first lunchtime one of them who'd spent the entire morning with the outside queues, told me he'd prayed with 12 people and taken one confession – and that he was in his element, doing the job he felt he'd been ordained for! People were coming from all over the UK – alongside the not insignificant numbers of overseas visitors who'd travelled to be in Leicester for the week. We counted 7,000 visitors on Monday and by the time we finally closed the doors after lunchtime on Wednesday over 20,000 people had filed past Richard's coffin.

The lengthy queues did present us with a problem – both logistical and pastoral. How would we manage them all, and keep them happy? Then I saw the goodwill and good working spirit not only of the cathedral team but all the central diocesan staff based at St Martins House come to the fore. Organising those queuing into orderly rows in a safe and fair manner was the least of our challenges, but certainly one to be managed – with team members walking up and down informing people of what was going on and how long they'd have to wait, and others sorting out tea trolleys and sweets to provide refreshment. My colleague Canon Rosy Fairhurst had a great idea to help the chaplain team respond to people's spiritual needs, based on the idea of lighting a candle, but adapted for the open air. Between the cathedral and St Martins House is a stretch of railing, punctuated by openings for pathways across. It's what's left of the old school railings, when the area was a playground.[53] Next to these they set up a series of baskets containing ribbons, in different colours, to represent different sorts of prayer – Please, Thank you and Sorry. The idea was to tie a ribbon of your

---

53 Ironically we had very much wanted to have that stretch of railing removed, to open up the space further, but the conservationists had argued successfully that we should only be allowed to make essential openings in the listed iron railings. As it turned out, to our advantage!

*The railings near the cathedral are covered in prayer
ribbons - Thank You, Please and Sorry.*

choice to the railings, as you silently voiced your prayer. And
if you wanted to, to speak to a chaplain, who might help you
pray it. Over the next few days those railings became a mass
of colour, as many people took the chance to bring to God
the deeper feelings that may have been stirred by the events.
Meanwhile, Bishop Tim also took the chance to move up and
down the queue speaking with people, who in turn very much
appreciated the opportunity. The whole experience, which could
so easily have been a logistical and public relations nightmare,
turned into a great time for almost everyone who was part of
it. The only edgy moments came at the end of Monday, as we
tried to enforce an 'end of queue' point, beyond which those
waiting wouldn't get into the building before we had to finally
close for the night by 9 pm. Some people who'd travelled a long
way, having seen the news on the television, seemed determined
they would get in regardless of what was said about volunteers
needing to get home after an immensely long day, and whatever
signs were put up telling them they were past the end of the
queue for the night. We got by with a combination of formal

stewarding, uniformed clergy on the scene and a lurking police presence in the background. And many of the hundred or so who in the end didn't make it that night were back early the next morning for a hastily arranged 7 am opening time, and got in easily enough then. But overall, most people spoke warmly of the friendly reception they'd received from our staff and volunteers as they queued – at its height up to four hours – and the fascinating conversations they'd had with people who, like them, had gathered for this unique opportunity to "be a part of history in the making" as so many put it.

The other big event on at the cathedral on Monday evening was a special service for members of the Richard III Society, held at 7 pm. We'd agreed this with their chairman Phil Stone months before, realising that there was no way we could recognise the special place Richard III holds in the hearts of members of the Society by the number of invitations available for the main services – although they did have a limited number allotted them at each one. So 700 additional invitations were sent out for an Evensong in the Presence of the Mortal Remains of King Richard III –conducted by the Dean and Fr Alan Hawker, a local Anglican priest who was himself a long-term Society member, with Bishop Tim preaching. Alan and I had largely composed the service, working jointly with Phil Stone, but I left the leading of it to him, David and Bishop Tim, being content to sit at the back and observe. As with so much of the week, my real rewards came from seeing what we'd planned for so long carried out to such great effect. At the end, when we gave Society members a chance to pass by the coffin and take their photos, such was their enthusiasm there was a difficult moment as cathedral staff had to link arms around the coffin to prevent it being overwhelmed and even toppled to the ground – which would have been the ultimate irony. But we needed to encourage them to leave as promptly as possible, since the queue outside was still gathering in number, as detailed above!

Tuesday and Wednesday followed a similar pattern of friendly crowds filing past the coffin from when we opened as early as possible until closing time. We had determined that even these unusual circumstances should not stop the cathedral's normal pattern of services of morning and evening prayer, said quietly in our new Chapel of Christ the King, and a Eucharist open to the public at 1 pm. We not only kept those prayers going, but also supplemented them so that every hour on the hour those filing past in the queue were asked to stand still whilst we led them in prayer, with a short time of silence, concluding by an invitation to join in with the Lord's Prayer – which we saw nearly all were glad to do. The 1 pm services were a bit different, as they were not about filing past the coffin to pay respects, but joining in with the worship that takes place every day in the cathedral. We arranged separate queuing for those, which were led by Bishops Tim and Christopher on Monday and Tuesday, and on Wednesday the short homily was given by Fr David Rocks, leader of the Roman Catholic Benedictines at Holy Cross Priory, and the Eucharist itself celebrated by Sister Beverley, an Anglican Franciscan priest. Also on Tuesday our normal evening prayer was replaced by Vespers, its Roman Catholic equivalent, led by a group of most of the Benedictine Monks of England, who had gathered at Holy Cross in Leicester for the occasion. It was very moving to see them process in for that service, followed by a crowd of their own congregants – but a bit of an organisational nightmare fitting everybody into seats, alongside the moving line of people still filing past the coffin!

By the close of Wednesday lunchtime's service, it was time to prepare for the momentous day to follow. The TV crews moved the rest of their kit back in, and by late afternoon a full rehearsal for the next day was under way. I also needed to oversee a different sort of rehearsal. Richard had been the last king of England to die in battle, leading his troops in defence of his crown, and in recognition of that the Ministry of Defence had agreed that the events of the next day were sufficiently momentous that they would provide us with an escort of serving troops. There'd been a preliminary recce a few weeks earlier, but the men involved reported to us for duty that Wednesday afternoon. We spent an instructive hour or so practising the technicalities of lifting and placing back down, and then lowering into a grave the replica coffin we'd had made by our Funeral Directors, filled with sandbags to the required weight. And as if that wasn't enough, following evening prayer came our first rehearsal *in situ* of Friday's Reveal service, with a hundred or so dancers recruited and rehearsed by Leicester's very successful provincial theatre, Curve, many of them coming into the cathedral for the first time.[54] That one I remember as particularly chaotic – but we had more pressing things on our minds at the time.

For most of the week I'd felt able to commute from my home on the southern edge of the city to the cathedral – but for this night and the following one I needed to be on the case throughout, and David had kindly agreed to let me sleep in a guest room in his Deanery, next door to the cathedral. So after a late meal with David, his family and guests, I rolled into bed around midnight, ready to rise with the lark the next morning.

'Reinterment' – Thursday 26 March

Thursday began early, as we celebrated our daily Eucharist at 7 am in the Chapel of Christ the King – and it was my turn to

---

54   The planning of this event was one of the first tasks for Curve's Nikolai Foster. Working to our brief, Nikolai along with choreographer Mel Knott had produced an amazing production in a very short time.

lead. The opening verse of the set reading for the day has Jesus telling his hearers: "Very truly, I tell you, whoever keeps my word will never see death." It felt a very appropriate reminder of the faith in which Richard lived and died – and which we were still there to celebrate and proclaim 530 years later.

The Archbishop of Canterbury, Justin Welby, and our three royal visitors were arriving later in the morning, but otherwise by 8 am everybody else was in place for our final run-through for the day before the service itself, due to begin at 11.30 am. Outside the crowds were once again gathering behind barriers – the skies were cloudy with a threat of rain, but that didn't dampen the enthusiasm. The coffin, of course, had already been in the cathedral since Sunday evening, but to mark the significance of this event we had arranged for a number of the more prominent guests to assemble in the Guildhall next door, and then to arrive in a series of processions between 10.30 am, by which time all other invited guests had to be in place, and 11.15 am, when we would be readying ourselves to receive the Countess of Wessex, representing the Queen, and the Duke and Duchess of Gloucester. These processions were mustered by Julian Haywood, and I didn't envy him the task. They included our full set of Bosworth Peers,[55] along with a number of carefully traced descendants of the ordinary soldiers who had fought on that fateful day; key members of the Richard III Society, the Dig Team and other dignitaries from the university; the people whose DNA had aided the identification of the remains, both Michael Ibsen and his family, and Wendy Duldig, but also a group of male-line or female-line DNA relatives; a group from the Bosworth area, both young people and representatives of the local church and

---

55 The current head of each of the relevant noble Houses traceable back to the Wars of the Roses had been identified, with the help of the College of Arms, and invited, and almost all were able to attend. A full list of those present is in Appendix 5 (p114). Of the 20 attending, 10 represented those actually present at Bosworth.

parish councils; and the members of the Cathedral Quarter Partnership Board, which had held ultimate responsibility for the whole event. The lining up and marshalling all went well. We'd been watching the forecasts carefully all along, as mid-March is a chancy time at best for English weather. In fact it had been brilliant all week, but Thursday was the one day rain was forecast, possibly heavy. We had contingency plans in case it was bad, but in the event the early drizzle eased off, and by the time the processions started it had just about stopped. Just after 10.30 am a military band, drawn from regiments whose history extended back to the Battle of Bosworth Field, marched to the front of the cathedral and before the eyes of a watching world[56] the reinterment of Richard III was under way, painted in the persons of those entering the cathedral.

Channel 4 had been interviewing their own panel of 'experts', some of whom had to be smuggled into the building at the last minute. There was a frisson of excitement as Benedict Cumberbatch was escorted over to take his seat next to Robert Lindsay, another actor who'd played Richard III. At the last, the royal guests arrived, were duly greeted and escorted to their seats, and on the dot of 11.30 am the service was ready to begin. As with the Reception service, the full text is available elsewhere; here I can only describe how it felt as I watched, from the frontest of front-row seats, the culmination unfolding of momentous events that had overtaken the past two years of my life. The coffin, of course, was still by the font at the west end of the church, by now with the pall removed and having on it only a small cloth, quartered in Richard's colours, with a fresh version of the floral tribute used on Sunday, and assembled behind it was the cathedral procession, myself included. The service began as we stood

---

56 Channel 4 began their coverage at 10.10 am and estimated a worldwide audience for the day in excess of 6 million people.

there with a eulogy to Richard, read by Professor Gordon Campbell, the university's public orator. Gordon had also been a member of the Liturgical Group planning the services, and is an expert in medieval English history and literature. He had also drafted the substantial Historical Introduction printed in all the service books.[57] At the conclusion of the eulogy, the army bearers marched forward and shouldered the coffin, and processed it to the centre of the cathedral, before the altar-table. In a moving moment, the Duke of Gloucester was then handed the actual copy of Richard's Book of Hours (prayer book), discovered in his tent after the battle, and which had later ended up in the library of Lambeth Palace, the London home of successive Archbishops of Canterbury since then, and placed it reverently on a small table next to the coffin. Later in the service he was to bring it into the ambulatory, where it remained as a poignant personal possession of the former monarch present as his coffin was lowered into his final resting place.[58]

The service proceeded with readings and a sermon by Bishop Tim – surely to the largest audience he'd ever preached to. Then the culminating action, as the soldiers stepped forward again, shouldered the coffin one last time and carried it through the screen into the ambulatory followed by the Archbishop, Bishop Tim, a senior Roman Catholic representative,[59] the royal guests – and the cathedral clergy. Once again I found myself within feet

---

57   At the very last minute we had discovered two small factual errors in this Introduction, which those few valiant web-warriors who still opposed Leicester took no end of glee in pointing out. All the books had been printed and it was too late to do anything other than apologise, which we did on the Project's website.

58   The Book of Hours, catalogued at Lambeth as MSS 474, is a priceless item, and was taken immediately after the service to Leicester's New Walk Museum, which had the necessary facilities to display it safely. It remained there for two months, before returning to the Palace library. A facsimile version, however, remains on display in the cathedral.

59   It would have been the Bishop of Nottingham, the Roman Catholic diocese which contains Leicester, but that post was vacant at the time so instead his senior representative, Fr Thomas McGovern, took the place.

Overseen by Justin Welby, Archbishop of Canterbury. The coffin of Richard III is lowered into his new grave. I am on the far left – looking very serious!

of the remains of Richard III as they reached the culmination of their long 530-year journey. It was close enough for me to note, with some anxiety as the soldiers side-stepped the coffin into position, that the feet of one of them were overlapping the edge of the graveside, but to my relief (and doubtless his) his balance remained, and no disaster ensued.

As the coffin was lowered into the grave, Archbishop Justin uttered the time-honoured words "earth to earth, ashes to ashes, dust to dust, in sure and certain hope of the resurrection to eternal life" and sprinkled into the grave soils gathered from three key moments in Richard's life – his birth at Fotheringhay, his adolescence at Middleham and his death on the battlefield now known to be at Fenn Lane Farm.[60]

Following that we returned to the central sanctuary for the final part of the service. Carol Ann Duffy's poem 'Richard' had

---

60   The porcelain containers in which the soils came to us were made by local artist Perrin Towlson, and stayed at the cathedral. They can be seen in one of our displays – and still have some of the soil in them.

its first public reading, and as the horns rang out the stirring introduction to Judith Weir's new setting of the National Anthem, my thoughts were at one and the same time conscious of the immense national significance of what I'd just witnessed and immensely relieved that everything had gone as planned.

After the service, we'd arranged for our honour guard to attend the edges of the ambulatory, to keep the tomb secure, as many of our guests pressed forward to see better what lay at the heart of what had just taken place before their eyes. We needed to clear the building – some guests to hospitality in St Martins House, others doubtless to the various hostelries of the town – so that we could prepare for the next day's events!

The Service of Reveal was to be even more of a performance in the more usual understanding of the word, and the team at Curve had arranged for an 8-metre-high sculpted installation to form a centrepiece of that event. This was due to arrive by lorry at the north door at 1 pm precisely, to be brought in and put in place in time for our next full run-through, scheduled for 3 pm. It not only needed erecting, but first of all hundreds of coloured roses had to be inserted into two massive circular discs which stood at the top of the sculpture. This was done by our amazing floral team who had worked their socks off all week, and now completed this near-final task. At the same time TV crews needed to remove large amounts of cameras and lights, which they had now finished with. It was tight, but we did it, and by 3 pm were all ready to rehearse the Reveal. The previous day's run-through had not gone well, so it now needed to start to come together. But it didn't. By 5 pm Johannes and Nikolai agreed the best thing to do was to send the dancers and liturgical team back home and start again in the morning. Because the next crucial piece of action was about to begin – the bringing of that tombstone into the cathedral.

The tombstone arrives

The sun was starting to set over St Martins House on a beautiful spring evening as the large lorry hired by stonemason James Elliot to bring the tombstone pulled up slightly later than scheduled, around 7 pm. He'd had problems even getting to us: with the large cross incised deep into its middle, the stone was delicate, and transporting it the 30 miles or so to Leicester was a challenging task in itself, not helped by the fact that a road closure due to an accident had meant having to use a pot-holed farm track for part of the journey. But here they were, with a handling crew ready to take it the final perilous journey into the cathedral and lower it into place.

There'd been quite a lot of delicate negotiating needed prior to this moment between James, Alex (his film-maker) and Rachel, the Channel 4 Executive Producer, about what could and couldn't be filmed. Channel 4 had a live programme scheduled for 8–9 pm to wrap up the day, introduced by their anchor presenter Jon Snow, and they were desperate to show the 'setting of the stone into place' as a live culmination of their coverage. James, however, had been adamant from the start that he couldn't promise that, in part because he had no real idea how long the process would take, and so where it would be up to in that one-hour slot, and in part because the processes and procedures involved were very delicate, and the last thing he – and we – wanted was for something to go wrong live on camera. We, of course, were equally clear that although we wanted to work with Channel 4 to show as much as possible of the events live, the most important thing was to carry it out properly – and if that meant no cameras at certain moments, then that was how it would need to be. So we'd finally reached a point where it was agreed that the unloading of the stone outside the cathedral was in public space, and could properly be filmed, but anything inside was out of bounds. Channel 4 had also wanted to wrap up its coverage for the day with some 'as live' footage from the ambulatory with David as Dean, Philippa and John from the Looking for Richard Project, and Michael and Wendy as the 'DNA relatives'. Since David was adamant that this should not involve other people making speeches in our cathedral, especially following the solemnity of a burial, it had been agreed to film a cameo introduced by him, with the others lighting candles in the Chapel of Christ the King and placing them by the grave, and then retreating into the dusk. I was looking on from the shadows as it was filmed around 6 pm, and following a couple of takes it all looked very impressive when it went on air as part of that 8–9 pm programme presented by Jon Snow.

Arrangements for the unloading of the stone proceeded, but by the time we reached 8 pm it was still on the lorry, with the camera crews along with a handful of interested members of the public watching from behind barriers. Josh was there, fully absorbed in the intricate process; David was elsewhere, being the Dean with assorted dignitaries – which left me representing the cathedral as events unfolded live before us. I had Rachel's personal mobile phone number, and as she directed the live programme from the TV truck across the road I rang her with progress updates from the spot, advising when and how the cameras might go live to the process. Between us, we managed to put out a show involving the staged 'end of day' moment, studio interviews and commentary – and the live movement of the stone into the cathedral. As the show came to its end we were still just manoeuvring it through the doors and into the cathedral.

The problem was taking 2.3 tonnes of stone safely across a newly laid floor, through a narrow entrance in the Nicholson screen into the ambulatory and then lowering it precisely onto the bedding of soft lead around the plinth on top of the vault. To do it James used a good old-fashioned block and tackle, a series of rollers and the manual handling skills of the two dozen crew members he'd brought along. By 10 pm it had been managed into the right place – and shortly before midnight I was able to text David, "The eagle has landed". It still took several hours more before the whole was bedded in to James' satisfaction and the last people left the building around 4 am.

Before that I'd taken time out to join the DSP and Channel 4 teams, along with our Comms people, who were gathering to celebrate a week's work well done. Although Rachel and others from a core group had been on the job for many months, for the week itself a large team had been assembled from specialists from all over the place – and now they were letting their hair down. There was champagne and cheering; there were speeches and thanks. The head of Channel 4 was elated – and told us all so. And then Rachel took me aside to say that genuinely everyone involved was agreed this was one of the best projects they'd ever been involved with – both in terms of content and also technical production. It perhaps was all summed up in the quote from Jon Snow in the aftermath: "I don't know of another city or another cathedral that could have done all this as well as Leicester." But for us, it wasn't over yet!

'Reveal' – Friday 27 March

Another morning dawned bright – the early rain of yesterday not repeated. It began in the cathedral with a short media opportunity at 7.30 am for photos of the tombstone in place on top of the grave. Our morning Eucharist followed at 8 am, and by 8.30 we were into a final rehearsal for the Reveal service. With a night's sleep behind us, and buoyed up by the success of the previous day, last evening's difficult rehearsal seemed left well behind, and everything seemed to fall quickly into place. By 11 am our final set of invited guests were streaming into the cathedral, this time with a strong representation from all aspects of the city and county's diverse communities, for a 12 noon start to the final great service of Reveal.

If the mood on both Sunday and Thursday had been full of the dignity and honour we had set out to create, it was clear that by Friday the city was more ready to celebrate – not indeed the death of a king, but the successful achievement of the unique feat of his reinterment with dignity and honour over half a millennium after that death came to be seen as marking the end of medieval England and ushering in the era named for the dynasty of his conqueror, Henry Tudor.

The atmosphere was lighter as people gathered. Security was much more relaxed with no live royals to protect, and the checking of invitations was at the cathedral door, not on the edge of an outer cordon. The civic and cathedral processions formed up and moved to our places, and a very different sort of service followed on – based around the themes of Conflict, New Beginnings and New Life. Each part was made up of a hymn or song, a reading and then one section of the performance from Curve members, which combined music,[61] dance and mime, taking up the whole of the space of the cathedral between the seated members of the congregation, and using to the full that 8-metre-high sculpture which stood either side of the plinth to the west of the sanctuary under the tower. It's not possible to do justice in mere words to the nature of what followed – but its culmination consisted of dancers removing from the tomb a large quartered cloth which had been placed over it, so 'revealing' it, at least to those seated in the chapels either side.

---

61 The music was both modern and traditional. It can't be often cathedrals have echoed to the rhythms of bass and drum, alongside the words of Revelation 21:1-4 set to music – "Then I saw a new heaven and earth".

*Dancers from Curve uncover the tomb as part of the service
of Reveal.*

Utterly moving to me, seated as I was under the tower, was a
moment in that dance when a young performer took Bishop
Tim by the hand, led him from his place in his new cathedra
to the sculpture, and urged him to insert a coloured rose into
its heart, symbolising the new peace we were all being called to
live for. Bishop Tim was first surprised and then visibly moved
as he joined in with great enthusiasm.

David preached a sermon calling us all to strive to build
the more compassionate and diverse society that the service –
and our city in its best moments – called us to, and at the end
we sang the words of that last and most joyful of the Psalms,
Psalm 150, to C.H.H. Parry's setting *Laudate Dominum*
– "O praise ye the Lord, praise him in the height." Then
everybody was invited to file past and view the revealed tomb
for themselves, before being handed by one of our wonderful
floral team, as they were leaving, a rose to take out into the
city – neither white nor red, but one of many other colours.

It felt magnificent to be there, and to know I'd had a part in bringing it all to pass.

Of course more frantic activity followed. As another 200 guests headed off for their hospitality, and the remainder into the city clutching their roses, myself and a team of staff and volunteers needed to turn the cathedral around, ready for the first of the public, who had patiently begun to queue outside to see for themselves the new tomb and new cathedral in all their glory. And by just before 3 pm we were ready, with chairs cleared, the pall in its display case, and the rope barriers up to marshal our guests around the preferred route. And they came. And came. And came. The final act of the day was billed as 'Leicester Glows', and had been arranged by the city.[62] From early morning a team had been putting around 8,000 outdoor candles in place in Cathedral Gardens, Jubilee Square and the streets around the cathedral – some on the ground, others in trees and in 'fire sculptures'. From 4 pm they were being lit, and as dusk settled the whole area took on an almost magical quality. The crowds re-gathered – local people alongside many visitors from elsewhere in the UK and all around the world – and wandered, almost entranced, in this mystical place that Leicester and its cathedral had become. By 5 pm I was able to place myself 'off-duty' and joined by my wife, we too wandered the streets around the cathedral.[63] I found it hard to take in that this was our city, our place, that had just witnessed such amazing historic events.

Then at 8 pm on the dot the roof of the cathedral was lit up by the start of an amazing firework display. I knew all

---

62   Masterminded by The Big Difference Company, the same group who 30 years earlier had started off what is now the famous Dave's Leicester Comedy Festival.
63   I had hardly been at home during that week – indeed Sue later said she had seen me more on TV than in the flesh!

Fireworks explode from the roof of the cathedral, and candles burn in the Gardens, as thousands celebrate a task well done.

about that too, as Emma, Peter Collett and I had been up on the roof a couple of weeks earlier with the company charged with installing the fireworks, looking at how best to do it, and in gaps in the previous couple of days' programme they had been up there again putting their equipment in place. We stood, two amongst the crowds that were by then tightly packing the area before the cathedral, shoulder to shoulder, and ooh-ed and aah-ed with the best of them. Projected onto the cathedral in lights, as it had been all week, was the Project's RIII logo, and at the very end it rose up to rest on top of the cathedral spire. Leicester glowed indeed. Leicester had done itself proud. And at the heart of it, central to the whole story, not just now but for the centuries to follow, was its cathedral. And I had, for a brief period, been able to be central to that. It felt very complete.

CHAPTER NINE

AND AFTERWARDS...

There's always an afterwards, and often it's not as uplifting as the main event itself. But in our case, I think perhaps it has been.

Our immediate afterwards was Holy Week and Easter, when we were able to combine all the traditional services the church has always held in those most special days with the great numbers of visitors wanting to 'see the tomb'. To start with it was running at around 7,000 a day, and by the end of the summer was still averaging 5,000 a week.[64] By the end of 2015 around 250,000 people had visited the place of Richard III's reinterment – and that's not counting those attending any of the many acts of worship that regularly take place. It has plunged us into a whole new phase of the life of our cathedral – what we started to call 'the new normal'. We knew it would be so – but nothing could easily have prepared us for what it means. Almost a year on, we're still coming to terms with that.

Not long after Richard's remains were first uncovered, and shortly before I joined the cathedral, a report had been

---

64 Compared with maybe 400–500 visitors on a good week, before the discovery of Richard.

published jointly by the Grubb Institute and Theos Think Tank, called *Spiritual Capital*. It was based on research in English cathedrals, which are one of the places where both in numbers coming and other measures people are showing ever-increasing interest in the Christian story. Many larger minsters and historic cathedrals have long known the challenge we now face – of people coming to view the place as tourists, but less interested in matters spiritual. The report said that there could be a tendency to separate cathedral visitors into two categories: tourists, coming to view architecture and the history, and pilgrims, looking for a more spiritual experience. This, the report suggested, was a mistake. Every visitor was somewhere on a spectrum where interest in history and buildings sat alongside a capacity for what we call 'the spiritual' which is in every person. Cathedrals do better to respond to those visiting not by dividing them into 'pesky tourists who pay the bills' and 'godly souls who we need to nurture', but rather meeting everybody where they are, but at the same time looking to offer something more. Especially so in a place dedicated in past and present to prayer and service, we should be glad of each visitor, and see if they might leave with that spiritual part of them encouraged into a little– or maybe a lot – more life than when they came in. We have trained our new legion of volunteer guides to this end; we have produced interpretative displays based on the life of Richard that seek to relate it to 21st-century questions about living, dying and what may lie beyond; we are building on the role of chaplains 'loitering with intent' to pick up on the prayers, needs or just desire for human contact that many bring with them. And the number coming to our services, every day and every week, begins slowly to grow.

Meanwhile, tourist bodies report that the 'Richard III phenomenon' has brought growth to the local economy, and put Leicester and Leicestershire firmly on the tourist map.

The City Mayor, Peter Soulsby, was re-elected on 6 May for a further four-year term with a resounding majority. And in the traditional East Midlands rivalry with our neighbours, the very real historical figure of Richard III begins to eclipse the more mythical, if romantic, image of Robin of Nottingham, just to the north. All of that is no doubt very good and necessary.

But what about our story – that of a cathedral church dedicated to prayer, service and proclamation to and for its many and varied communities? Cathedrals nowadays, like other major institutions, benefit from having a Strategic Plan, and since the reinterment we've been working hard on ours. There's plenty of thinking gone on in there, but we've summed it up in one simple sentence: *Leicester Cathedral – a beating heart for city and county.* Of course, our very geography means that we sit at the heart of both our city and our county – two very different but interdependent entities, themselves located at the geographical heart of England.[65] But more than that, Christian faith is at the heart of all we do. And in a city, and world, where many faiths and other world-views make many claims, we've worked hard to show that our belief is in a God who loves all of his created world, and offers hope to all people. Although in a very different age, it's still the faith by which King Richard III lived and died. And everything about his 21st-century tomb proclaims that it's a faith that offers hope beyond this life as well. It's in a place of continuous prayer, and as our many visitors come to see where this last medieval king lies, and light their candles, offer their own prayers and tell us their own stories, we believe we're simply telling another chapter in a Story that runs down the ages and across the universe.

It's too early to say what the final impact of the Richard story might be on Leicester Cathedral, but I am convinced that

---

65 There's a field a few miles to the west of Leicester, and not so far from Bosworth, with a stake in it, that reckons to be placed at the geographical dead centre of England. Who's to disagree?

by sticking to our guns, by determining to rebury this former monarch with dignity and honour, on behalf of a nation, but without compromising anything of our central Christian beliefs, we can only be better off. Certainly David Monteith has started this part of his life in the church in a way few if any of his fellow deans can hope to rival!

And as for me? I've had an amazing time. I've met some fascinating people. And I've witnessed close-up and been integrally part of a chapter of English history that people will write about for generations to come. What could possibly top that?

APPENDICES

Appendix 1: Official letter to Cathedral asking to reinter remains

Please ask for: Peter Soulsby
Direct line: 0116 252 8313
Our ref: 2013/Jan/CN/PS/MH
Date: 28 January 2013

Leicester
City Council

Reverend Canon Barry Naylor
Acting Dean and Urban Canon
Leicester Cathedral
St Martins House
7 Peacock Lane
Leicester
LE1 5PZ

Dear Barry

Reinterment of remains, potentially of King Richard III, in Leicester Cathedral

I am writing on behalf of Leicester City Council and the University of Leicester to let you know that the remains potentially of King Richard III, were exhumed on 5 September 2012 by the University of Leicester Archaeological Service in Leicester City Council's Grey Friars car park. They were taken into the care of the University of Leicester, for study as part of the excavation project. Once these studies are complete, both the University of Leicester and Leicester City Council agree that these remains should be reinterred in St Martin's Cathedral Leicester, in line with the Ministry of Justice exhumation licence relating to them.

This intention was discussed in 2011 with Vivienne Faull, who was the Dean at the time, should such remains be found, and had her approval before the application was submitted.

We are very pleased to hear you support this proposal, along with Bishop Tim Stevens and the Cathedral Chapter. I would be most grateful if you could confirm this in writing to Richard Buckley, the Ministry of Justice's licence holder, copying your response to Sir Bob Burgess and me. Richard Buckley of the University of Leicester Archaeology Service can then arrange for the transfer of these remains to you in due course.

Yours sincerely,

Peter Soulsby
City Mayor

cc: Sir Bob Burgess, Bishop Tim Stevens

OFFICE OF THE CITY MAYOR
Peter Soulsby

7th Floor, B Block, New Walk Centre, Welford Place, Leicester LE1 6ZG
TELEPHONE (0116) 252 8313   themayor@leicester.gov.uk   www.leicester.gov.uk

Appendix 2: Early Project Structure diagram

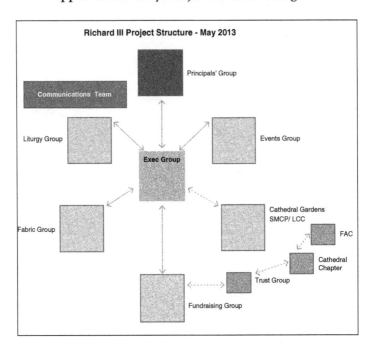

Principals Group: Tim Stevens / The Dean, Professor Sir Bob Burgess, Sir Peter Soulsby, Jennifer Lady Gretton

Executive Group: The Dean (Chair), Prof Mark Thompson (UoL), Sarah Levitt (City), Mike Smith (BL), Tim Webster (Lieutenancy), Pete Hobson

Communications Team: Liz Hudson (Diocese), Chris Taylor (City), Jon Shears (UoL) Richard Taylor (UoL)

Fundraising Group: Claire Recordon, Elizabeth Amias (For information), Liz Hudson, Pete Hobson.

Liturgy Group: Johannes Arens (Chair), Chris Johns, Christopher Woods, Tim Stratford, Alan Hawker (Riii), Liz McKenzie (City) Prof Gordon Campbell (UoL)

External Consultants: Jonathan Goodall, Alexandra Buckle, Julian Litten, DavidStanicliffe

Cathedral Gardens Project Board: John Nichols, Rafe Cherry (SMCP); Andrew Smith, Andrew Shillingham, Barry Pritchard (LCC). In attendance Pete Hobson, Louise Seymour

Fabric Group: Mandy Ford (Chair), Sally Henshaw (Riii) Dr Sally Tarlow (UoL), Janet Arthur (Chapter)

Events Group: Pete Hobson (Chair) Maggie Shutt (City), Jon Shears (UoL), Charlotte Barratt (UoL), David Potter (Riii), police (tbc)

Appendix 3: List of Pete's Blogs

All available (at date of publishing) on the website kingrichardinleicester.com
under the News tab, as Cathedral Blog

2014		Title	Trigger for the reflection
31 Jan	1.	Lessons from my daughter's graduation	Attending the graduation ceremony of our daughter at the University of Sussex
7 Feb	2.	Team 101 – what we're really all about	The work of The Prince's Trust in SMH
14 Feb	3.	A man that looks on glass …	A line from George Herbert's hymn, about finding God in the everyday things of life
28 Feb	4.	Cathedral life in 3D	A 3D model, created to help explain our proposed alterations to CFCE and others
7 March	5.	Inspired by love and anger	A line from an Iona-inspired hymn about what moves me …
14 Mar	6.	Richard III has his day in court	Judicial Review, round two
21 Mar	7.	The ambassador comes to town	A visit to the cathedral by the American ambassador
28 Mar	8.	Watching and waiting	The uncertainty, awaiting the outcome of Judicial Review
31 Mar	9.	The people from CFCE say "Yes"	Approval of our plans by CFCE
14 Apr	10.	Yorkshire Post, you make us smile	A knocking campaign against Leicester run by the Yorkshire Post
17 Apr	11.	It's not about right and wrong	How we argue, in the light of Easter
27 Apr	12.	Ricardians – we salute you	Ricardians met in the course of this process
3 May	13.	Rev – real or pretend?	The TV programme 'Rev'
15 May	14.	Dying matters	A joint conference between the cathedral and the university on how we deal with death down the ages
24 May	15.	You must be very pleased	Initial reaction to the outcome of Judicial Review
4 June	16.	What are they saying? What are we thinking?	Further reactions from others to Judicial Review
14 June	17.	Towards Stillness	Explaining the new sculpture in Cathedral Gardens based on Richard's story

22 June	18. Now we're getting going	A busy period as various plans get turned into action
29 June	19. "Goodwill, cooperation and reconciliation"	Words used to characterise a recent meeting between Project staff and Richard III Society
6 July	20. How does your garden grow?	Cathedral Gardens is officially opened
2 Aug	21. Perspective	On coming back from holiday in Northumberland
25 Aug	22. March 26th 2015 – hold that date	Announcement of the date of the reinterment
26 Aug	23. Stories of the Stones	Stones inside the cathedral moving to prepare for reinterment
7 Sept	24. Friends and colleagues	Relationships within the team
15 Sept	25. Appearance – and reality	The photo version of the Nicholson screen
21 Sept	26. Of rocks and rivers	Choosing the stone for the tomb
4 Oct	27. Memento Mori	The bodies found beneath the cathedral floor
12 Oct	28. A busy old week	A lot of project activity!
19 Oct	29. It was a dark and stormy night	A talk given at Bosworth Battlefield Visitor Centre
2 Nov	30. The Bosworth Peers	Introducing the concept
17 Nov	31. Behind the scenes in the Cathedral	Where the work is up to
6 Dec	32. Leicester welcomes the public at large	The process for asking to be invited to the services
21 Dec	33. How many want to come?	Response to the above
2015		
7 Jan	34. Now we're motoring	New Year activity
18 Jan	35. Singing it out loud	Musical contribution to an invited event
31 Jan	36. Welcome to the stone roses	Floor tiles with the carved white roses arrive
15 Feb	37. 14th Feb is love your cathedral day	Valentine's day, and a cathedral cleaning day
1 Mar	38. It's all coming together	Final preparations
8 Mar	39. Let's hear it for James Elliott	The tomb designer
22 Mar	40. On your marks, get set ...	At the start of reinterment week
28 Mar	41. Richard Reburied – he is now	At the end of reinterment week

Appendix 4: Revised Project Structure diagram

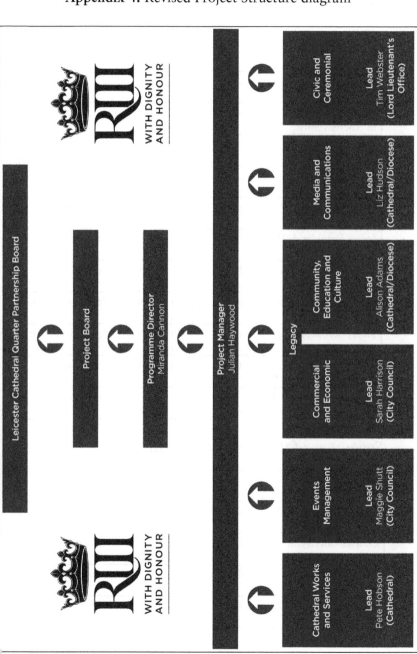

Appendix 5: Full list of Bosworth Peers, and original titles

Edward Howard, 18th Duke of Norfolk	Sir John Howard, 1st Duke of Norfolk
David Manners, 11th Duke of Rutland	Sir Robert Manners of Etal
Christopher Nevill, 6th Marquess of Abergavenny	Lady Anne Neville
James Stourton, on behalf of 27th Baron Mowbray	Anne Mowbray, 11th Baroness Mowbray
David Herbert, 19th Baron Herbert	William Herbert, 2nd Earl of Pembroke
Robin Devereux, 19th Viscount Hereford	Sir Walter Devereux, Baron Ferrers of Chartley
James Frankland, 18th Baron Zouche	John la Zouche, 7th Baron Zouche
Richard Cornwall-Legh, 6th Baron Grey of Codnor	Henry Grey, 4th Baron Grey of Codnor
Harry Orde-Powlett, 8th Baron Bolton	John Scrope, 5th Baron Scrope of Bolton
Harry Scrope, Scrope of Danby	John Scrope, 5th Baron Scrope of Bolton
Ralph Assheton, 2nd Baron Clitheroe	Sir Ralph Assheton of Middleton
John Wake, on behalf of Sir Hereward Wake, 14th Baronet	Roger Wake of Blisworth, Northamptonshire

Supporters of the House of Lancaster

Geoffrey Somerset, 6th Baron Raglan	Lady Margaret Beaufort
Edward Stanley, 19th Earl of Derby	Thomas Stanley, 3rd Baron Stanley
Charles Chetwynd-Talbot, 22nd Earl of Shrewsbury	Sir Gilbert Talbot of Grafton
Charles Courtenay, on behalf of 18th Earl of Devon	Sir Edward Courtenay of Tiverton
Alexander Fothergill, on behalf of 8th Baroness Braye	Sir Reginald Bray of Eaton Bray, Bedfordshire

Other Connected Persons

Thomas Woodcock, Garter King of Arms	College of Arms incorporated in 1484
Peter O'Donoghue, York Herald	College of Arms incorporated in 1484
Richard Dannatt, Constable of the Tower	Sir Robert Brackenbury, Constable of the Tower **

* Present at Battle of Bosworth
** Killed at Battle of Bosworth

Lightning Source UK Ltd.
Milton Keynes UK
UKHW02f1431121117
312604UK00007B/103/P